TORCH BIBLE COMMENTARIES

Genesis 1–11

GENESIS 1-11

ALAN RICHARDSON

SCM PRESS LTD

COLLEGII BEATAE S. HILDAE DVNELMENSIS
PRINCIPALIBVS MAGISTRABVS STVDENTIBVS
QVARVM AMICITIA HOC DECENNIO VSVS EST
HVNC LIBELLVM
DEDICAT AVCTOR

© Alan Richardson 1953

334 00538 8
First published 1953
by SCM Press Ltd
58 Bloomsbury Street London WC1
Eleventh impression 1979
Printed in Great Britain by
Fletcher & Son Ltd, Norwich

CONTENTS

5

III

PREFACE

This volume aims at providing a theological commentary upon the first part of the Book of Genesis. That is to say, its chief purpose is to elucidate the significance of Genesis 1-11 considered as Holy Scripture or as the revelation of divine truth. Christians believe that God speaks to us through the Scriptures of the Church, and it is with the divine Word spoken to us in Genesis that we shall be concerned.

But God's Word, though addressed to us here and now, was given through the mouths of men who lived centuries before our time. Accordingly two tasks are imposed upon the commentator. First, he must show, with the aid of every resource of biblical scholarship, how the divine message was received and understood by the original hearers long ago; and therefore we have tried to sum up as concisely as possible just so much of the critical, historical and literary discoveries of modern Old Testament research as is essential for a truly historical understanding of Genesis. And secondly, he must show how the ancient truth of Genesis is to be received to-day in an age which, not surprisingly, tends to look to modern science for an account of the world and of man, their beginnings and their possibilities; and therefore we have tried in the Introduction to describe the nature of religious truth, such as is given to us in the parables of Genesis, and to show how it differs from and does not conflict with scientific truth. In this way it is hoped that the difficulties and misconceptions which arise for the ordinary reader when he turns to the opening pages of the Bible will be removed.

To those familiar with the literature of the subject it will be obvious that the author is indebted to many writers besides those mentioned in the Bibliography. One particular debt must be acknowledged: the Rev. G. Henton Davies, M.A., B.D., B.Litt., Professor of Old Testament Studies in the University of Durham, has kindly and patiently read through the whole work in manuscript. While he is not to be held responsible for the judgments expressed in these pages, his criticisms and suggestions are responsible for many improvements upon the version which first came into his hands.

ALAN RICHARDSON

The College,
Durham,
Lady Day, 1953

BIBLIOGRAPHY

S. R. Driver, *The Book of Genesis*, Westminster Commentaries, Methuen, London, 1904 (and subsequent editions).

J. Skinner, *Genesis*, International Critical Commentary, T. and T. Clark, Edinburgh, 1910.

W. H. Bennett, *Genesis*, The Century Bible, T. C. and E. C. Jack, Edinburgh (n.d.).

S. H. Hooke, *In the Beginning*, The Clarendon Bible, Old Testament, Volume VI, Oxford, 1947.

W. Vischer, *The Witness of the Old Testament to Christ*, Volume I (Eng. trans. from 3rd German ed., 1936), Lutterworth Press, London, 1949.

C. R. North, art. ' Pentateuchal Criticism ' in *The Old Testament and Modern Study*, ed. H. H. Rowley, Oxford, 1951.

G. von Rad, *Das erste Buch Mose*, Kap. 1-12.9, Das Alte Testament Deutsch, Vandenhoeck und Ruprecht, Göttingen, 1949; 2nd Ed., 1950.

The Commentary is based upon the Revised Version of 1884 (RV) and its margins (marg.), though sometimes reference is made to the Authorized Version of 1611 (AV). EVV indicates a reference to both these English Versions. LXX stands for the Septuagint Greek translation. O.T. stands for Old Testament; N.T. for New Testament. Following the usage of the RV, where the Hebrew text has Jahweh (Jehovah), LORD is put in capitals.

INTRODUCTION

THE PLACE OF GENESIS IN THE JEWISH CANON OF SCRIPTURE

The title 'Genesis' is a Greek word meaning 'origin', 'source' or 'begetting', and it was used as a superscription for the book in the Greek Bible (i.e. the Septuagint, usually referred to by the sign LXX). Thence it was adopted into the Latin Bible (i.e., the Vulgate) and so into the English Versions. As a title the word was doubtless suggested by the first theme with which the book deals, the creation or 'genesis' of the world. The actual word occurs in 2.4 in the LXX version: 'the book of the *genesis* of heaven and earth'. The Palestinian rabbis called the book *Bereshith,* which is the opening word of the Hebrew Bible and means 'in the beginning'.

Genesis constitutes the first of the five divisions or books into which for the sake of convenience the rabbis divided the Law (Heb. *Torah*). These first five books of our Old Testament (Genesis, Exodus, Leviticus, Numbers and Deuteronomy) are collectively called the Pentateuch (Gk., *pente*, five; late Gk., *teuchos*, a book), and were the earliest part of the scriptural writings to become the Bible of the Jews (during and after the days of Nehemiah and Ezra); they were, indeed, the only part of the Bible to be recognized as entirely authoritative by *all* Jews even as late as New Testament times. To this original nucleus of the Law (*Torah*) were added first 'the Prophets' and later 'the Writings'; but even in the days of our Lord the Sadducees looked upon the Prophets and the Writings in the same way as the Reformers

looked upon the books of the Apocrypha: they were not to
be used for the establishment of doctrine but only 'for
example of life and instruction of manners'. The absolute
authority of the Pentateuch (*Torah*) was in part based upon
the belief, universal by New Testament times, that it had
been written down by Moses himself; our Lord is represented by the evangelists as adhering to the view that
Genesis was the work of Moses (Matt. 19.3ff.; Mark 10.3ff.).
Belief in the Mosaic authorship of the Pentateuch became
traditional in the Christian Church and survived until the
rise of modern biblical research in the nineteenth century;
hence sprang one of the traditional names for Genesis, 'the
first Book of Moses'.

It is impossible to overestimate the significance and value
of the *Torah* in the eyes of a devout Jew in our Lord's time.
The *Torah* was his source of instruction upon every question
of belief and action, of religion and daily life. It was his
daily meditation and delight, whether in public worship or
private devotion. But it was also the foundation of his
nation's existence, the record of his people's origin and calling, as well as the basis of all their social morality and
legislation. If we wish to overhear something of the over-
tones which the word *Torah* contained for the pious Jew,
we should read carefully Psalm 119, that long-sustained
expression of the joy of a soul that is ravished by the love
of God and of his Law; but we must remember that the
word 'Law' is not entirely adequate as a translation of
Torah, which means, besides law, instruction, guidance,
helpful direction, teaching—always implying the presence
of God as Counsellor, Helper, Guide and Friend. Thus to
understand something of what the *Torah* meant to the Jew
will help us to appreciate the place of Genesis in the Canon
of the Jewish Scriptures. Amongst the rabbis it was sometimes given the honourable title, 'one of the five fifths of
the *Torah*'.

THE PENTATEUCH IN THE LIGHT
OF MODERN RESEARCH

In order to understand how Genesis was compiled we must
have some idea of the composition of the Pentateuch as a
whole in the light of modern knowledge. It is now no longer
open to us to suppose that Moses wrote the Pentateuch, for
it has become abundantly clear that the whole of the Five
Books, as they now stand in our Bibles, has been put together
by an editor (or, more probably, by a number of different
editors) who made use of several separate sources. These
sources themselves were composed by various authors (or
collectors of traditional material) at widely diverse times and
places, under a wide range of different social and political
conditions, and with markedly divergent interests and aims
in view. In short, Genesis, like the other books of the
Pentateuch, is a composite work. There is only a general
consensus of opinion amongst scholars about the nature,
date and provenance of the sources of the Pentateuch, and
we must not be surprised at their failure to agree about
many matters in a sphere where the evidence admits of a
variety of interpretations. The whole study is a fascinating
exercise in literary and historical criticism, and one which,
in view of the wealth and complexity of the knowledge now
available, requires a lifetime's application. Amongst other
things it presupposes a sound knowledge of Hebrew and
other Semitic languages. But happily for our purpose of
theological elucidation, we can gratefully take the broad
results of the devoted labours of scholars in this field and
use them with due deference to the principles on which they
are based—much as we may take and apply in our everyday lives the results of the electrician's specialized knowledge,
without being ourselves expert electricians or physicists.
We must remember that behind the theological enquiry into
the books of the Bible there lies a vast range of technical and

specialized knowledge, which must never be pre-judged or forced or swept aside in order to facilitate a theological short cut. In this section we will try to sum up just so much critical information as is essential for our purpose.

Since 1885 the dominant theory has been that there are four principal sources of the Pentateuch (though there are also other lesser sources). These have come to be denoted by the letters J, E, D and P. J, so called because it character-istically uses the divine name *Jahweh* (*Yahweh, Jehovah*), and was held to be a document comprising ancient Hebrew traditions written down somewhere in the Southern King-dom of Judah and sometime during the monarchy, probably after the time of Solomon. E, which characteristically uses *Elohim* as the name for God, is a not very dissimilar collec-tion of the traditions of Israel, emanating in all probability from the Northern Kingdom of Ephraim at some date not much later than that of J. In due course these two docu-ments, J and E, were conflated by an editor to form JE. D was the work of the Deuteronomic school which instigated the attempted reformation of the cultus associated with the discovery of a ' Book of the Law' in the Temple in 621 B.C. during the reign of King Josiah (II Kings 22). P stands for the Priestly Document, the work of exiles returning from Babylonia in the fifth century, upon which was based the whole development of post-exilic Judaism associated with the names of Nehemiah (*c.* 444 B.C.) and Ezra (*c.* 397 B.C.). The editorial activity which combined these quite different elements into the Pentateuch, as we now know it, belongs to the period of quiet reconstruction during the years of Persian dominance after the time of Nehemiah. Such, in its simplest and barest outline, was the generally accepted critical theory of Pentateuchal origins at the beginning of the twentieth century.

Some modification of this general theory will doubtless have to be made in the light of subsequent research. It is now suspected that each of the strata, J, E, D and P, so far

from being originally a document written by a single author
(or compiler of traditions), is at least as complicated in its
origin and construction as the older critics conceived the
Pentateuch itself to be. Indeed, it has been doubted,
especially in Sweden, whether J, E, D and P were ever
documents' at all, and it has been suggested that they
were rather ' streams of (oral) tradition '. One thing at least
seems fairly generally agreed: it is impossible to date these
sources as belonging to or confined within any particular
period. Each of them represents a current of tradition or
way of thinking which persists throughout Israel's history,
so that it is a mistake to regard J as belonging wholly to the
tenth and ninth centuries or P as belonging only to the post-
exilic period. Even if we postulate—as British scholars on
the whole still seem to think that we must—an author of
J who flourished during the tenth or ninth century B.C., we
must remember that not only was he a collector of earlier
traditions but also that after his time several additions may
well have been made to his work. Similarly, it must be
conceded that, even if P as a whole is post-exilic, it in-
corporates very much older elements and exhibits a type of
mind and of tradition that has existed all down Israel's
history: P has closer contacts both in language and religion
than have any of the other Pentateuchal sources with the
recently discovered Ras Shamra material, which yields contemporary evidence about the cultus and myths prevalent
in Palestine in the fifteenth century B.C.

Those who wish to consider in greater detail the present
position of Pentateuchal criticism are recommended to con-
sult Professor C. R. North's essay on that theme in *The
Old Testament and Modern Study*, edited by H. H. Rowley
(Oxford, 1951), or, more briefly, the art. PENTATEUCH
in *Chambers's Encyclopædia* (new edition, 1950).

THE SOURCES OF GENESIS
1-11: J AND P

Of the four main Pentateuchal sources we are concerned
only with J and P, since E and D do not appear in the first
eleven chapters of Genesis. It is essential that we should
be familiar with the distinction between J and P, since the
recognition of these two sources solves the problem created
by the duplication of (or in) certain of the narratives (e.g. the
Creation and the Flood) and by the discrepancies which
appear between them. The later editor(s) of the Pentateuch
has used his sources in different ways at different points;
thus, he has allowed the two Creation stories to stand side
by side (Gen. 1.1–2.4a, P; and Gen. 2.4b-25, J), without
attempting to conflate them; whereas in the Flood story he
has (somewhat clumsily) combined his two sources (see commentary *ad loc.*). When we have firmly grasped the truth
that Genesis is compiled from quite different sources, we
shall no longer be perplexed by the discrepancies between
certain statements. For instance, in the P narrative of the
Creation we read that man and woman are created simul-
taneously after the creation of fishes and birds and beasts;
whereas in the J narrative we find that the order of the
creation is first man, then the animal world, then woman.
Nor shall we regard such divergences as perturbing, because
(as we shall see) the Creation stories are not to be looked
upon as scientific accounts of how the world came into
being. Again, we sometimes find discrepancies in what
seems to be a single consecutive narrative: for instance, in
the story of the Flood we read alternatively that two
creatures of every kind of beast, clean and unclean, are to be
taken into the Ark (6.19; 7.8f.), and that seven pairs of clean
beasts and one pair of unclean beasts of every kind are to
be taken into the Ark (7.2f.) Here the conflation of sources
accounts for the confusion; the direction to take one pair

comes from **P**, and the direction to take seven pairs from **J**. It is unnecessary to cite further instances.

J and **P** are clearly and easily distinguished from each other by their characteristic differences of language, style and theological standpoint. Differences of language do not always appear in our English versions, just as we would hardly expect to find quite the full variation of vocabulary between (say) Milton's *Paradise Lost* and Eliot's *Waste Land* in a French translation of those works. Nevertheless differences of style and outlook are easily perceptible to the attentive English reader.

THE CHARACTER OF J

The style of **J** is simple and child-like, but his insights into the character of God and the nature of man are profound and adult. He—we will speak of **J** as 'he' for the sake of brevity—reflects deeply upon the world as he finds it, upon human existence and social institutions, upon nature, animate and inanimate. All these things he relates to God, for he sees their meaning only in relation to their divine Creator. The older commentaries used to tell us that **J** was a 'pre-scientific' thinker, and that, not knowing the scientific account of the origin of things, he satisfied his natural curiosity by inventing mythical 'explanations' of the phenomena around him: how the world came into existence, why there are different sexes, how it happens that people are conscious of guilt, why they wear clothes, why hard work is unpleasant but necessary, why serpents crawl on their bellies, what is the origin of the institution of marriage, of polygamy, of agriculture, of viniculture; why mankind is divided into nations, speaking different languages; how a proverb originated (10.9; 22.14); why there was a curious pinnacle of salt overlooking the Dead Sea (19.26)—and so on indefinitely. 'The explanations offered of these facts,'

says S. R. Driver (*Westminster Commentary*, p. xvii), 'are
not historical or scientific explanations, but explanations
prompted by religious reflection upon the facts of life.'
Other commentators have been less kindly (and less per-
ceptive) even than this. They have dismissed the 'explanations' offered by J as mere legend and make-believe which
can be cleared out of the way now that we have a scientific
attitude towards the phenomena which J observed. The
logical end of this unbiblical way of thinking is to dismiss
J's (and therefore the Bible's) whole conception of God and
man from our 'scientific' world-view. Why do we need
to retain the 'pre-scientific' notion of a Creator now
that we have such up-to-date concepts as 'creative evolution' or 'continuous creation', and why do we need any
explanations of sin beyond those that Marx and Freud can
give?

The truth is that J was not seeking explanations at all.
He had no conception of historical and scientific explanation
in the modern sense, and to attribute such scientific leanings
to him is anachronistic. He knew as well as we do that
snakes do not crawl on the ground because an ancestor of
theirs spoke ill-advisedly in the Garden of Eden. J was not
making childish guesses at the origins of things at the level
of primitive science and primitive history. He was reflecting
upon the nature of things, not as objects of curiosity or
scientific interest, but as incidents in the encounter of man's
soul with God. His stories are parables, not explanations.
He uses parables of nature and of man in order to convey
deep religious insight. We must think of J's stories as akin
rather to the parables of the Lord Jesus than to the explanations of things put forward by the genuinely pre-scientific
Greeks—Thales and Heracleitus and the pre-Socratics
generally. J is emphatically not a Hebrew Pythagoras.
Many modern folk are misled on this matter by their failure
to understand that the language of religion is the language
of parable and poetry, and that ultimate truth can be

expressed and communicated only by means of the images
and symbols of the imagination, not by the exact prose of
the scientific intellect. By ultimate truth we mean truth
about God and man's relationship to him, truth which none
of the sciences deals with—or professes to be able to deal
with. The deepest levels of truth, truth concerning our
existence, cannot be articulated in the prose of scientific text-
books. To say this implies no slur either on science or on
religious truth: it is merely to point out what is so often
forgotten, that they are different things. It is the difference
between scientific truth and what we shall call existential
truth, that is, truth about our existence in relation to the
world as a whole, to other persons, and to God. (This distinction is dealt with more fully below.)

Thus it often happens that the apparently artless sim-
plicities of J are considered by sophisticated modern folk to
be childish speculations and fables, which can be left behind
(along with Santa Claus and Jack-and-the-Beanstalk) once
the adult (or scientific) stage has been reached. Such an
attitude implies a conception of truth which is completely
unbiblical and utterly mistaken. The J writer is not childish
but child-like, in the sense which our Lord declared to be a
pre-condition of entry into the Kingdom of God: 'I thank
thee, O Father, . . . that thou didst hide these things from
the wise and understanding, and didst reveal them unto
babes.' We must learn to think of the stories of Genesis—
the Creation, the Fall, Noah's Ark, the Tower of Babel and
the rest—in the same way as we think of the parables of
Jesus; they are profoundly symbolic (though not allegorical)
stories, which are not to be taken as literally true (like the
words of a text-book of geology), but which yet bear a
meaning that cannot be paraphrased or stated in any other
way without losing something of their quality of existential
truth. To take them literally is to spoil them and miss their
truth just as certainly as to look upon them as 'pre-scientific
explanations'. Both taking them literally and dismissing

them as legends are errors of spiritual adolescence; it is not
the J writer who is immature, but the sophisticated people
who have not reached an adult perception of the nature of
religious symbolism and imagery. J certainly uses anthropomorphisms (Gk., *anthropos*, a man; *morphe*, form), that is,
representations of God in human guise. 'They heard the
voice of the LORD God walking in the garden in the cool of
the day.' But anthropomorphism is not a mark of im-
maturity, but of maturity; there are plenty of anthropomorphisms in the teaching of Jesus; it is the only way in
which a genuinely transcendent, infinite and ineffable Deity
can be characterized—and J is adult enough to know this.
To assume that J takes his anthropomorphisms literally—
that he really believed in a physical Deity who took an
evening stroll in the Garden of Eden—is purely gratuitous,
and it is entirely at variance with J's profound understanding
of God as the Maker of heaven and earth. Such an assumption arises from the 'evolutionary fallacy' which has vitiated
so much modern thinking and to which we must give further
attention below.

We have spoken above of J as a single person for the sake
of convenience; and indeed the fact that the J writings
everywhere bear the hall-mark of an astonishing religious
insight, at once child-like and profound, points rather to
one supreme prophetic mind than to a school of such
geniuses. But we must not dogmatize. It may be that in
the childhood of the race, before the stage of sophistication
was reached, this kind of vision of truth was more widespread than we might suppose; it may be—and there is
other evidence to support such a contention—that in the
early stages of man's development, when the traditions
which J has collected were taking shape, a profound
religious awareness of the nature and purpose of things was
'natural' to man, and that with the growth of civilization,
when the shades of the prison-house were beginning to close
around our race, a certain 'fall from grace' was taking

place, whereby man's pristine vision was obscured. Certainly the vices, the artificiality, the sophistication and the luxury of civilization, of which ' primitive ' man knew nothing, cannot but have darkened our native human perception of the inner meaning of things. Hence, at this stage of civilization, the genuine prophet is a rare and lonely occurrence; he is usually in revolt against the culture and civilization of his day; and it is significant that he characteristically looks back to an age of innocence and forward to a day of redemption, when the prevailing and obscuring illusions of an age of false standards do not exist.

J (whether man or group) is essentially a prophet. He differs from the great prophets of the eighth and following centuries in that he is not (in the sense in which they were) in rebellion against contemporary civilization. He is rather the mouthpiece of an inward awareness shared by many in preceding generations and doubtless in his own. This is not to say that many of his ideas and practices are not naïve and even superstitious if judged by the fuller knowledge of later ages; but then, every age, including our own, has its full share of naïveties and superstitions; credulity would seem to be a constant factor in all ages of history. But in spite of many things which we should regard as primitive crudities, there seems to have been something more akin to ' open vision ' in his days, even though we must guard against the romantic notion that there ever was a time when all the Lord's people were prophets; the study of the contents of J would make it apparent that any such assumption is false. Nevertheless J does exhibit that kind of direct insight into the fundamental human situation *vis-à-vis* God which was at a later date the possession of the great prophets of Israel, although there is a difference. What is that difference? In the less developed social structure of an earlier age the social vices against which the eighth century prophets thundered had not arisen, and so J's perception of judgment and redemption is not so stark, so poignant, so

agonizingly experienced as was theirs. But it is present
nevertheless. It is present in the way in which the trustful
obedience of childhood is the precursor of that deeper
fidelity of the manhood which has been tested and tried
amidst the fierce struggles and bitter failures of later life.
Revelation (as the Bible understands the matter) comes
through trustful obedience to the will of God; and in this
sense J is an 'inspired' writer and the bearer of divine
revelation. He prefigures the whole biblical revelation: he
knows of the one true God—for other gods he cares nothing
—who has made him and all the world, before whom every
man stands convicted of rebellion, to whom every man is
responsible. But he knows also of a God who will not let
man go, who will punish but will not annihilate, and who
has a purpose of mercy and love for the whole human race.
This purpose he has perceived embodied in the history of
his own people, through whom all the nations of the earth
will be blessed. The outcome of human life and history
may be safely left in the hands of such a God as this; the
forces of evil and the consequences of man's rebellion will
some day be done away. This much he knows, because the
promise of victory is inherent in the quality of God's loving-
kindness which he and his people have experienced. Therefore through God's aid man's rescue and redemption are
guaranteed. Or, to use his own dramatic way of expressing
such matters, the seed of the woman shall bruise the
serpent's head.

THE CHARACTER OF P

Though, as we have seen, P gathers up a long line of
tradition stretching back through Israel's history, it is nevertheless clear that the work as a completed whole belongs to
the period of (and after) Nehemiah and Ezra. P stands on
the other side of the great crisis of Old Testament history,

and is separated from J by some five centuries of time and by the prolonged, catastrophic period of upheaval caused by the invasions from the North-East (Assyria and Babylonia), a period which culminated in the destruction of Jerusalem (586 B.C.) and the exile in Babylon. During this whole period, which may be said to have begun when Amos (c. 760 B.C.) first prophesied judgment and disaster, all the great prophets of Israel did their work. It was among the aweful and purifying fires of judgment that the Word of the Lord came to the prophets who declared to their bewildered and unperceptive fellow-countrymen that their God had not abandoned them but was chastening them, that the disasters which had overtaken them had not occurred because he was weak but because he was strong and righteous, that his purpose was unchanged and irresistible, and that it must go forward inexorably until the Day of the Lord. This long period of crisis was the time of the testing, purging and deepening of Israel's religion. Taught by the prophets, the Remnant that finally was left to rebuild the nation's life was faced by the daunting task of re-establishing the worship of Jehovah and the laws and customs of his people upon the pure and uncontaminated doctrine of the holy and righteous God as the prophetic movement had enunciated it. This was the task associated with the names of Nehemiah and Ezra. It is unnecessary for our purpose to determine what was the precise relation of P to the 'Book of the Law of Moses' which Ezra the priest read from his wooden pulpit before the water-gate from early morning until midday (Nehemiah 8). The important point for us to grasp is that the finished P belongs to this period of reconstruction and consolidation, though it must be remembered that the P tradition then gathered and re-presented stretches back to the earliest days of Israel's history.

Sometimes too much is made of the alleged conflict between prophet and priest in the Old Testament, and some people speak as if there were a necessary opposition between the prophetic and priestly points of view. It is true that there was a bitter conflict between a prophet like Amos and priests like the priests of Bethel (Amos 7). But these were the old, unreformed priests who had corrupted the worship of Jehovah with borrowings from the immoral cultus of the heathen baals. By the end of the Exile the fires of judgment had purged them and their corruptions away. The reforms which had begun under Josiah (c. 621 B.C.) had borne little fruit before the whole edifice of Jewish social and religious life had been overwhelmed in the catastrophe of the invasion of the Babylonians and their destruction of Jerusalem. By the waters of Babylon the exiles did not merely sit and weep when they remembered Zion and the Temple; they planned and prepared for a new cultus to be erected on the basis of the old P tradition and on that of the theology of the prophets, notably Ezekiel. Thus, when after the rebuilding of the Temple (520-516) a new start could be made, the way had been prepared for a reformed Jehovah-worship such as was instituted by Nehemiah and Ezra, utterly purged of the corruptions of baal-worship and the heathenish immoralities of the old high places. The latter were everywhere desecrated, and the worship of Jehovah was now definitely and finally centralized in Jerusalem. P offers not only a programme for this reformed cultus but a whole social and legal system inspired by it. It has influenced and is itself influenced by the high doctrine of God which the prophets had enunciated. P includes a revised and re-written account of Israel's origin and history, beginning from the Creation of the world—a new, stream-lined, stylized history of Israel into which the ideals of the Priestly school are read back. The regulations which are to control Jehovah-worship and the laws which are hence-forward to govern the nation's life are attributed to Moses in the desert. Moses' tabernacle is an idealization of the worship that was now to be set up in Jerusalem, and so on. How much of the content of P is genuinely carried over from

pre-exilic tradition we must leave to the scholars to determine.
One thing is certain: P, as we now have it incorporated into
the Pentateuch, represents the broad agreement of the
faithful priests and lawyers of Israel with the teaching of
the prophets. Doubtless there is always tension between the
prophetic, reforming mind and the more conservative,
traditionalist type of the priestly mind; but it may be said
that in P we come as near to a resolution of this tension as
men are ever likely to achieve in the life of the Church
amidst the concrete actuality of history.

The P source runs all the way through the Pentateuch (and
beyond it through Joshua). In its treatment of the development of Israel's life and history P handles with loving care
such institutions as Circumcision, the Sabbath, the Passover,
the Feasts and Sacrifices, in which the Priestly school is
naturally very interested. P has a definite historical scheme,
which is scrupulously adhered to throughout. The divine
name Jehovah (*Jahweh*) is never used until after it has been
revealed to Moses—P's understanding of the matter is set
forth in Exod. 6.2f.—whereas in J it is used from the
earliest times. Since, according to P's scheme of history, the
sacrificial system was not instituted until the time of Moses
(the first recorded sacrifice in P is offered by Aaron in
Lev. 8), there is no mention in P of altars and sacrifices
in the Patriarchal period; whereas J, on the other hand,
makes frequent references to sacrifices in the days of the
Patriarchs. Many other such instances could be brought
forward to show that P offers a re-writing of the history of
Israel to fit into the Priestly conception of the economy of
revelation and of the right response that must be made by
God's People. In P's scheme of history there are four world-
ages: from the Creation to the Flood; from Noah to
Abraham; from Abraham to Moses; and lastly the Mosaic
age. It is in this last and culminating age that the theocracy
of Israel is set up: Moses builds the tabernacle, after the
heavenly pattern revealed to him; the Covenant with God

is inaugurated on Mount Sinai; the Law is given, and all the
details of the Mosaic cultus and morals are revealed and
declared binding for all time.

P's stylized history is matched by its formal and legal
literary style. Stereotyped phrases tend to be used whenever
possible, and everything is made as uniform as it can be.
Even in the first eleven chapters of Genesis, and in our
English Versions, certain words and phrases that will often
be repeated strike the ear: 'kind', 'after its kind', 'be
fruitful and multiply', 'after their families', 'and (Noah)
did according to all that God commanded', 'generation',
'these are the generations of'.

THE CHRONOLOGY OF GENESIS

To bridge the gaps between the high points in their story
the editors adopt the device of filling in the intervening
spaces with genealogies. This enables them to suggest the
passage of considerable periods of time, periods of which
they know nothing in detail. In this practice they are following the precedent of P (and probably J before him). The
study of the chronological systems which underlie the
various figures mentioned in Genesis, such as the ages of
the Patriarchs (e.g. 7.6, 11; 9.28) is very complicated and is
a fascinating pursuit for scholars, but it need not detain us.
It is sufficient here to remark that these figures are of no
historical value; there is a systematic divergence in the three
chief recensions of the text (the Massoretic, the Samaritan
and the Septuagint), so that it is not even possible to determine with accuracy what was the original chronology of P.
But it is clear that P's chronology was not consistent with
that of JE. Hence it is futile to attempt to estimate the
'biblical' date of the Creation of the world, or of the Flood,
or of any of the rest of the pre-historical material of Genesis.
As we shall see, these 'events' are not to be understood as

happenings on the plane of ordinary history. The attempt to reconstruct the beginnings of world-history from the primitive chronological data of Genesis is as foolish as the effort to produce a calendar for the end of the world from the Books of Daniel and Revelation. The dates which are found in the margins of some English Bibles—e.g. Creation, 4004 B.C.; the Flood, 2349 B.C.—are entirely valueless in the light of modern knowledge; they are based on the calculations of the learned James Usher (1581-1656), Archbishop of Armagh, who published the results of his researches in his *Annales Veteris et Novi Testamenti* in 1650; they were first added to the English Bible by Bishop Lloyd in the great edition of 1701. Scientists find it difficult to estimate the age of our earth, but they have little doubt that some rocks are over 1,500,000,000 years old!

THE PARABLES OF GENESIS

The chief interest of Genesis 1-11 is centred in what we have called the 'parables'—the two Creation Stories, the Fall, Cain and Abel, the Flood and the Tower of Babel. Sometimes these stories are called 'myths', but this word is open to serious misunderstanding. In everyday speech a myth is a fable, a mere legend: one might say, for instance, that the story of King Canute at the Wash is 'only a myth'. There is, of course, another use of the word familiar to scholars, namely, to signify a story which is not literally true but which nevertheless contains a deep philosophical meaning, like the myth of the Demiurge in Plato's *Timaeus*. If one could assume that everyone would understand the word in this scholarly sense, it would be less objectionable to speak of the stories of Genesis as myths; but there is a further consideration. If we speak of the 'myth of the Creation', we are using language which inevitably suggests that there was no real act of creation at all, whereas this is

not what we should mean. God *did* create the world: this
is no myth. Similarly man's condition *is* fallen: there is,
alas, no question of myth here. The most that we can with
propriety say is that the accounts of the Creation and Fall
in Genesis are *mythical in form*; but since there is the ever-
present danger that we shall be understood to mean that the
Creation and Fall are 'only myths', it is perhaps better to
avoid the word altogether. We have adopted instead the
word 'parable'. This word has the advantage of not necessarily implying that the happening to which it alludes is only
a fiction. When Jesus speaks the Parable of the Mustard
Seed, the word does not imply that mustard seeds do not
really grow—a conclusion which would surely be implied
if we spoke of the 'myth' of the mustard seed. A parable
is a story which may or may not be literally true (no one
asks whether the Good Samaritan ever literally 'happened');
it conveys a meaning beyond itself. It implies that beyond
the words of the story which our outward ears have heard
there is a meaning which only our spiritual hearing can
detect: 'he that hath ears to hear, let him hear'. Again, a
parable is not an allegory; it is not a tale in which *every*
object mentioned stands for something else; it has just *one*
'point', one total implication. It is the meaning of the
parable as a whole that is the important matter. (The
allegorical or figurative interpretation of Holy Scripture was
much practised by the Fathers of the Ancient Church, but
it is not one which can be followed by biblical theologians
to-day; see further on this question the present writer's
Christian Apologetics, London, 1947, pp. 180ff.)

It is of the utmost importance to realize that the parables
of Genesis are to be read in the way that we read poetry,
not prose. Their language is as far removed as possible
from that of a scientific text-book. They make use of poetic
images and symbolism, which must be treated as such. We
must read them as, for example, we would read Shakespeare's imagery:

> '. . . Look, how the floor of heaven
> Is thick inlaid with patines of bright gold:
> There's not the smallest orb which thou behold'st
> But in his motion like an angel sings,
> Still quiring to the young-eyed cherubins. . . .'

We can, if we wish, complain that Shakespeare's cosmology is pre-scientific, pointing out that modern astronomy does not support the view that heaven has a floor, and that therefore the suggestion about patines of bright gold must be regarded by modern folk as wishful thinking: the whole mediæval notion of the music of the spheres must be discarded in the light of modern discoveries in astro-physics. If we heard criticism of this kind, we should be quick to call nonsense by its proper name. Surely these are amongst the loveliest lines in all literature, and the truth which Lorenzo is expressing has nothing whatever to do with modern astronomy; nor does it matter one iota whether Shakespeare believed in a three-storey universe or not. Yet unimaginative criticism of the above kind is often met with in discussions of Genesis, and many people find it hard to think of the parables of Genesis as masterpieces of the poetic imagination. But this is exactly what they are, and by the imagination they must be approached.

The poetic images that we find in Genesis are those which recur continually all through the Bible. The Bible has its own universe of poetic symbols, and if we do not enter sympathetically with the imagination into that universe we shall not understand the Bible as a whole or Genesis in particular. Light and Darkness, the Creative Word, the Chaos of the Deep, the Firmament of Heaven, the divine Image, the first Adam, the One Flesh of Man and Woman, the Serpent, the Tree of Life, the Covenant of God with Man, the Altar of Sacrifice, the Paradisal Garden, the Babel-confusion of mankind—all these images, and many more, which meet us in the early chapters of Genesis, are amongst those very images by means of which the biblical revelation itself is mediated to us. Time and again in the biblical records they appear and disappear; then reappear under new forms and with new meanings; they melt away again, only to recompose themselves as the embodiment of a deeper understanding of the mystery of God's relationship with man. How sadly we shall misconceive this symbolism if we think of Adam as a real, individual man, or of Eden as an actual garden that once existed and could have been located geographically somewhere by the source of the Euphrates! We must realize that Adam, Eden, the Serpent, the Ark, and so on, are all poetical figures; they belong to the poetry of religious symbolism, not to history and geography. The truth with which they deal is not of the same order as the truth with which history and geography, astronomy and geology, deal; it is not the literal truth of the actual observation of measurable things and events; it is ultimate truth, the truth which can be grasped only by the imagination, and which can be expressed only by image and symbolism.

The kind of 'truth' which is contained in the Genesis parables is the truth of religious awareness. This truth cannot be stated in philosophical, theological or psychological terms, because that would be to transpose it into one of the other orders of truth, to de-personalize it. The parables of Creation do not offer us a theory, a philosophical hypothesis, of how the world came into existence; nor does the parable of the Fall offer us a scientific analysis of human nature. On the contrary, they offer me personal knowledge about my existence, my dependence upon God, my alienation from him, my need of reconciliation to him. Doubtless certain general truths about the whole universe or about the condition of human nature as such are implicit in the awareness of myself-in-relation-to-God which the Genesis parables awaken in me or communicate to me; but only if I have *first* perceived that this existential truth applies to *me*, shall

I comprehend that such general truths for philosophy and theology are involved in the Genesis stories. I must first understand that I am Adam, made in God's likeness, rebelling against his purpose, desiring to be 'as God'. The Genesis parables certainly carry many and deep implications concerning mankind in general, but I shall not understand this until I have first come to know that they are addressed to the particular Adam which is myself.

Religious awareness, if communicable at all through words, must be communicated by means of the poetic imagination, the poetic image. This is the way in which the biblical revelation comes to us. It does not come by way of intellectual propositions: an intellectual proposition (such as 'God is love') is an inference from the revelation through persons and symbols, not the content of the revelation itself. As is often said, it is Christ himself who is the revelation, not a creed about him, even though creeds are necessary to guard against false conceptions of Christ. Similarly in the parables of Genesis the revelation there given is not a series of propositions (such as that the world was created by God or that mankind is fallen), even though such propositions may rightly be inferred by those who know subjectively the truth of the revelation. This revelation occurs when, enlightened by the biblical words, I come to know that *I* am dependent upon God, was created by him, am responsible to him and stand convicted before him. The revelation as a present reality takes place here and now in my encounter with God through the words of the Bible.

Thus it is not the task of the commentator to paraphrase the words of the Bible. Often we find that people expect to be given a series of simple propositions which 'explain' to them in everyday language the 'message' of Genesis (or of the Gospels, or of the Bible). Such people are first cousins of those who ask to be given a simple 'explanation' of *The Waste Land* or *A Sleep of Prisoners*. The parables of Genesis must be heard, like all works of the poetical

imagination, in their own words or not at all. The school-
boy's paraphrase of the *Ode on a Grecian Urn* is not what
Keats ' meant' by it. The literary critic's analysis of *The
Waste Land* does not lay bare the ' message' of Eliot—still
less communicate the truth that Eliot saw. The commentator on the parables of J cannot epitomize in modern
language the ancient writer's insight. Biblical scholars,
however learned, cannot analyse for us the meaning of the
parables of Genesis, although they can be an enormous help
to us in supplying the essential background information
which enables us to relate them to the whole corpus of our
knowledge and experience—just as a visit to a cathedral or
an art gallery is much more profitable if we have a com-
petent guide. But in the last resort the stories of Genesis
must make their own impact upon us; they must speak to
us personally, so that we see for ourselves that the truth
which they communicate is true for us.

MYTH AND RITUAL

Long before the nomadic Hebrews had become a civilized
people, a common pattern of religious myth and ritual had
established itself throughout the ancient civilizations of the
Middle East. Its purpose was not so much to purvey religious or ultimate truth as to control the mysterious processes of nature—more particularly the fertility of the land
and the success of the harvest—upon which the life of man
depended. It was thus more akin to magic than to what
we (taught by the Bible) understand by religion. In nature-
religion the fertility-god is born in the spring and dies in the
autumn. At the Babylonian new year festival in the spring
the birth of the god was celebrated in an elaborate ritual
in which the king, taking the part of the god (Marduk),
engaged in a ritual combat with the chaos-monster (Tiamat),
while the epic or myth of this encounter—the Babylonian

myth of the creation—was recited by the priests. Then the victorious king-god took part in a solemn procession to his enthronement, and afterwards went through a ceremony of marriage with the goddess (his queen or a priestess). If this ritual pattern were not carried out, the crops would not grow, the population would not multiply and the cows would not calve. This kind of fertility-cult spread amongst all the agricultural peoples who surrounded the Israelites in Canaan; it seductively tempted them away from the austere and ethical worship of Jehovah; and so we find that the prophets from Elijah onwards maintain a constant thunder against the immoral cultus of the fertility-baals.

It is obvious that the J and P traditions of Genesis have completely transcended this fertility-religion, even though certain of the forms of their parables bear affinities with the Babylonian myths. It is because the stories of Genesis belong to a wholly different *genre* of thought and worship that the use of the word 'myth' in connection with them is out of place. In both J and P there has taken place a thorough-going 'demythologizing' of the Babylonian pattern, so that the biblical writers can use without fear of misunderstanding certain of the elements of the old myth (Creation-story, Flood-story, etc) or some of the old mythological images (e.g., God as king, or God as the spouse of Israel). But the biblical writers in making use of the old myths and images have stood them on their head; they have employed them in the service of a totally different conception of the relation of God and man. The biblical creation-stories were not designed as myths for recitation in a magical fertility festival: they show, not how God can be made to serve the purposes of men, but how men are utterly dependent upon God and are responsible before him for their every word and deed. Perhaps we can best understand the world of difference that lies between the Babylonian myths and the standpoint of the biblical writers if we meditate upon the completeness of the inversion which they effected, and if we

ponder the revolution which has taken place in the transition
between the two statements: 'The king is god' and 'God
is king'. Once this demythologizing revolution has taken
place, the great prophets of Israel themselves feel no
difficulty in making use of the images of the old myth (e.g.,
that of divine kingship); after the ritual has ceased, the myth
itself has no potency. Once the corruptions of the 'high
places' had been brought to an end, the biblical writers
could use the imagery of the myth for their own lofty purposes.

In the light of these considerations we should note that
neither the J nor the P school may be thought of as
'primitive' thinkers. Implicit in their work is an advanced
criticism of the genuinely primitive Babylonian myth-ritual
pattern, and, judged purely in the light of 'history of
religion' standards, they represent a highly critical and
developed viewpoint in relation to it.

SCIENCE AND GENESIS

When we understand the nature of the Genesis parables, we
shall no longer suppose that there can be a conflict between
'science' (i.e. the natural sciences) and Genesis. Genesis
is not a scientific account of *how* the world came into existence; if I want to learn how this happened, I must go not
to Genesis but to science. It is misleading even to speak of
Genesis as 'pre-scientific', for Genesis is not concerned with
scientific questions at all; it is not a collection of the guesses
of primitive men at answers to scientific questions. It is dealing with matters beyond the scope of science: its theme is
man's awareness of his existence in the presence of God,
his dependence upon and responsibility towards God. This
high theme is dealt with in the only satisfactory way in
which the human mind can deal with it, that is, in religious
symbols. We shall miss the whole point of Genesis if we

either take the parables of Creation, the Fall, and the rest, literally or look upon them as primitive guesses at scientific or philosophical truth.

It is partly because religious people themselves have not understood the nature of the Genesis stories, but have treated them literally, that the existence of an opposition between Genesis and science has been widely assumed. There is no reason, however, for the continuance of such a supposition to-day. But there is another and a more important reason, namely, the ambiguity of the word 'science' in its everyday usage. If we use the word (as we ought to use it, and as we have used it above) to mean science of the type of the natural sciences, then it is clear that there can be no conflict between science and Genesis, because the two are talking about different things. But if we use the word science (as we should not) to mean a particular philosophical theory, sometimes called 'the scientific attitude' or 'scientific humanism' but more properly called naturalism or positivism, then, of course, there will be a fight to the death between 'science' and religion. Though it is often called 'the scientific attitude' by its upholders, this point of view is not 'science' at all, but a very old kind of materialistic philosophy. The main tenet of this philosophy is that scientific truth is the only kind of truth; that is to say, that nothing which cannot be verified by the scientific method (i.e. the method of observation, induction, experiment and verification, as employed in the natural sciences) can be called knowledge. It follows upon this assumption that religious knowledge (or what we have called existential knowledge) is mere opinion or guess-work, since it cannot be verified by the scientific method. (Of course it cannot! God, because he is *God*, cannot be made the object of scientific observation.) There is a fatal objection to the view that any truth that can be known to be true must be capable of demonstration by the scientific method, namely, that this proposition itself cannot be demonstrated by the scientific method and must therefore be held to be 'mere opinion'.

One of the unfortunate consequences of the positivistic habit of mind, so widespread nowadays, is the uncriticized assumption (to which we have alluded above) that there was no knowledge of any value before the rise of modern science. The assumption is false, because the kind of knowledge that we have called existential possesses a value that is independent of date and an insight into truth that does not grow old. This is one of the main differences between it and what we have called (as a convenient short-hand term) scientific knowledge: in the sphere of natural science every new discovery means that an old hypothesis becomes obsolete and must be discarded. It is a positivistic error to think that the same is true in the sphere of existential knowledge. Were it otherwise, the plays of Aeschylus would be as out of date as the physics of Aristotle; Jeremiah's prophecies would be as irrelevant to our condition as the psychology of Protagoras, and the Dialogues of Plato would be as 'dated' as the astronomy of Ptolemy. But we know that the tragedies of Aeschylus, the oracles of Jeremiah and the Dialogues of Plato will always be read and will never be outmoded because our fundamental human existence itself has not changed: that which makes us *men*—beings who are defined by our basic relation to God and to our fellows—is just what it was in the days of the ancient dramatists, prophets and philosophers. The rise of modern science has not removed or modified the basic human predicament which the J writer understood so well; rather it has underlined it. Men still go to war or make love from the same motives and with the same passions as in the days of old; they marry and give in marriage as in the days of Noah. That is why the ancient dramatists, prophets and poets can tell us just as much about our real human existence as can the modern ones—and it makes no difference at all whether they believe in a Ptolemaic or a Copernican or an

Einsteinian cosmology, or, for that matter, whether they believe that the earth rests upon the back of an elephant standing on a tortoise! A great tragedy, a prophetic insight, a profound philosophy, open a window upon truth which the passage of time will never darken. We must at all costs avoid the superficial modern error of thinking that the law of evolution applies with equal validity to every aspect of our nature; it is a hypothesis which has proved useful primarily in the sphere of biological science, and if it is extended uncritically beyond its proper sphere it will give rise to endless delusion. It does not apply at all in the sphere of existential knowledge; in this sphere the later is not necessarily the higher and the ancient is not to be written off as 'pre-scientific'.

Before we leave this topic, one last word remains to be said, especially to those who are teachers of children or guides of youth. Teach, at whatever age the developing mind is able to grasp it, that there is a distinction between the truth of science and the truth of the poetic imagination. Never teach the latter as though it were the former. Otherwise the adolescent will dismiss Genesis along with Santa Claus and the other 'myths' of his childhood. Teach the Genesis stories to children by all means: there is nothing to be gained by waiting until the child is 'old enough' to absorb a technical exposition of the nature of poetic symbolism! But never teach the stories as literally true, or give the impression that they ought to be so considered, by your timidity in answering the natural questions of the growing mind. And by all means teach, along with your lessons on the Creation-narratives, the account of the physical origins of the universe as given to-day by leading scientific thinkers. It is not difficult to do this, even if we ourselves know nothing about modern science; there are a number of excellent 'popular' little books from which we can get up the subject adequately for our purpose in half an hour. Or go to the public library and read the articles on EARTH;

PLANET; EVOLUTION; MAN, EVOLUTION AND ANTIQUITY OF,
in *Chambers's Encyclopædia* (1950 edition). Teach the
modern scientific cosmology and the theory of evolution in
the Sunday School as well as in the Day School. This at
least can be done to save our pupils from receiving a shock
when some day they switch on the radio and hear some
Third Programme lecturer discoursing upon the latest scientific theories about the origins of the world and of man.

THE PLACE OF GENESIS IN THE CHRISTIAN SCRIPTURES

In what does the revelation enshrined in Genesis consist?
Not in the disclosure of any scientific knowledge (such as
we obtain from the natural sciences) about the origin of the
world or similar matters. Nor again is the revelation to be
equated with the promulgation of any philosophical ideas,
such as theism, or the hypothesis of the creation of the
world by God. The revelation given in Genesis, as we have
already said, consists in its communication of awareness of
our real situation, of the utter dependence of ourselves and
our world upon God, of our personal relationship to him
and to our fellow-men in all its intricate counterpoint of
rebellion and reconciliation. From this awareness many
conclusions for our philosophy are indeed to be derived, but
the biblical revelation is data for philosophy rather than
philosophy itself. According to the Bible we do not come
to God by constructing rational hypotheses about him; we
come to him, as to a Person whom we have encountered,
and whom to trust is to know. If we will not trust him and
obey his will, we cannot know him. It is the refusal to
trust God's Word and to obey his commandments which
causes men to be ignorant of him, to doubt his existence,
and to embrace false philosophies and pseudo-scientific
theories. Atheism is essentially a failure in personal relation-

ships. ' It is so hard to believe,' said Kierkegaard, 'because
it is so hard to obey.'

Genesis is an integral part of the total biblical revelation
which culminates in Christ and is homogeneous with it.
What we find in Genesis 1-11 is taught both implicitly and
explicitly in the rest of the Bible. God is the living God, the
almighty Creator of heaven and earth, who has made us, in
his wisdom, in such a way that our hearts will be restless
till they rest in him. He has created us in his own image
and likeness, even though as a result of our rebellion against
his purpose and through our desire to be ' as God ', the
divine image in which we were made has been sadly defaced.
Yet despite our defection, God has not abandoned us;
Genesis, like the rest of the Old Testament, is forward-
looking; it expects a new creation, in which a renewed Adam
shall re-enter upon that Paradisal state of peace with God
from which by his sin the first Adam was outcast. Genesis
is only the ' beginning ' of the story which the whole Bible
tells; the completed drama will unfold the mystery of God's
plan according to which he sent a Second Adam to the fight
and to the rescue, Jesus BEN ADAM, Son of Man, in whom
God's original image and likeness are whole and unimpaired.
Into the redeemed humanity of this Last Adam, the Christ
of God, we are incorporated when with repentance and faith
we are baptized into the Church which is his body. Genesis
is thus an integral part of the canon of Christian Scripture,
which contains the whole revelation of God to man. Like
every other book of the Old Testament it points forward to
Christ and cannot be understood apart from its testimony
to and fulfilment in Christ. The Church, which possesses
in Christ the key to the Scriptures, alone can give us the
true interpretation of Genesis.

In what, then, does the inspiration of Genesis consist? It
may be recognized by the ability of Genesis to communicate
the religious awareness of man's existence—of *our* existence
—in relation to God. Through this awakened awareness

God himself is speaking his Word to us, is addressing us. This awareness is communicated under the forms of image and symbol and parable. Poetic images do not 'date' or become outmoded like scientific hypotheses; the true, deep images at the very base of our human consciousness remain the same in all ages, though they clothe themselves in different forms at different times. We need not be afraid that the parables of Genesis will ever be outgrown, because our fundamental human existence does not 'evolve': man-in-relation-to-God-and-his-fellowmen is a permanent, not an evolving, relation. The images which Genesis (or the Bible as a whole) employs are the basic images of our existence as over against God; through them, when they become alive in our imagination, the revelation of God's character and purpose is imparted to us. Because, through its poetic symbols and basic images, Genesis has the strange power to confront us with the naked truth of our human predicament before the majesty and goodness of God, we may rightly speak of the 'inspiration' of Genesis. Why *this* book, written in *this* way, should have this mysterious power, we cannot say; it is part of the total mystery of divine revelation. Revelation is always the gift of God, vouchsafed where and when he will, and not as we might expect. All we can do is to thank God with humble adoration for his gift of Genesis, as of all Holy Scriptures written for our learning, and pray that we may in such wise hear them, read, mark, learn and inwardly digest them, that by patience and comfort of his holy Word, we may embrace and ever hold fast the blessed hope of everlasting life, which he has given us in our Saviour, Jesus Christ.

COMMENTARY

I

THE CREATION
1.1—2.25

The idea of ' creation '—calling into existence out of nothing
—did not first enter the human mind as a result of philosophical speculation. The Greek philosophers never arrived
at it. In the myth of creation in Plato's *Timaeus* the divine
Demiurge (lit. ' worker ', ' craftsman ') fashions the world
out of matter which is already *there* by imposing form upon
it, much as a potter makes vessels out of clay. To-day we
often speak of the work of a craftsman or artist as ' creative ',
but the Bible does not do so. Creation in the biblical sense
is *creatio ex nihilo*—out of nothing. It is utterly beyond the
power of man to perform; it is essentially miraculous, and
can be accomplished only by the living God, the God of
miracle (Jer. 32.17, RV marg.). Aristotle thought that the
material world must be eternal; he could not conceive how
matter could have had a beginning in time. The idea of
creation, now of course a well-known philosophical notion,
was originally a gift from revelation to philosophy, like many
other ideas (that of personality, for example).

If the Hebrew mind did not arrive at the idea of creation
by way of philosophical speculation, how then was that idea
reached? Jehovah was known to the Hebrews as the Lord
and Controller of history: through their experience of having been called and guided, protected and disciplined, amidst
the vicissitudes of their nation's life, the prophetic knowledge of God as the Lord of the nations had been attained.
The fertility-baals and the foreign deities were no gods at

41

all. The doctrine of God as the Creator of the whole world,
of all that exists, reaches its highest and most emphatic
expression in the Second Isaiah: 'Thus saith Jehovah that
created the heavens; he is God; that formed the earth and
made it; he established it, he created it not a waste; he
formed it to be inhabited: I am Jehovah, and there is none
else' (Isa. 45.18; read Isa. 43–46 continuously to savour the
fully developed prophetic consciousness of God's transcendent power and holiness as Creator). The Lord who had
been encountered in history was revealed to Israel as the
almighty ruler of the destinies of nations; and it was inevit-
able that the prophets should conclude that the world of
nature—the theatre and stage of history—was also his
handywork and empire. The P story of creation (Gen. 1.1–
2.4a) was, of course, written down as we now have it a
century or so after the time of the Second Isaiah; but many
scholars to-day are coming to think that the material under-
lying the P tradition is much older than the Exile and may
well have moulded to some extent the thought of the Second
Isaiah and his predecessors. The J story of creation
(Gen. 2.4b-25) is, of course, much older than Amos, and
proves that the prophetic insight into the nature of God
as Creator was current in Israel even before the days of
Elijah.

Alongside of Israel's encounter with God as the Lord of
history we must set another factor in the development of the
biblical knowledge of God as Creator. There was also the
deeply religious awareness of standing in the presence of
God, recognized as the source and ground of one's own
existence. The God revealed in their nation's history was
revealed to prophetic minds in Israel as the 'thou' over
against whom the 'I' is defined. This awareness includes
consciousness of dependence upon God, of creatureliness
in the presence of the Creator, of being responsible to him
for all one's thoughts and words and deeds. Such an awareness is compellingly present in the J narrative of the Creation

and Fall, and, unless it is communicated to us as the truth of our condition—the basic fact of our existence—we shall not have understood the deep meaning of that narrative. This sense of creaturely dependence upon God and of responsibility before him is, of course, present throughout all the books of the Bible; notably we find it in the magnificent poetry of Job 38-41. Unless I know that I am created by God, am utterly dependent upon him, am responsible to him and am judged by him, the creation of the world will be for me only a philosophical speculation (even though I may regard it as intellectually the most satisfying hypothesis about the world's origin and *raison d'être*) or merely a ' dogma ' of the Creed (even though I may assent to it as the teaching of the Church). To know that God made *me* (and *therefore* all the world) is to understand the parables of Creation aright; it is this kind of ' existential ' knowledge which the Genesis stories of the Creation can communicate to us or awaken in us. When they do so—when I can say that they are true *for me*—then I know that God has spoken his word to me through them, and they are indeed for me *sacred* scriptures.

(a) THE FIRST CREATION STORY
1.1—2.4a; P

The distinctive character of the P Creation Story is displayed not only by the stylized phrases, often repeated, but by the whole Priestly conception of the created world as the scene of the manifestation of the glorious majesty of God—' even his everlasting power and divinity ' (Rom. 1.20). The universe as God planned and made it is like P's ideal Tabernacle : everything in it reflects the glory of God ' after its kind '—sun and moon and stars, day and night, trees and herbs and grass, beasts and birds and fishes—everything performs its duly ordained liturgical office, like the priests and levites of the sanctuary in their appointed courses. And

finally man, as the arch-priest and crown of the whole
created world, exercises dominion under God in this vast,
cosmic theocratic empire, in which everything that happens
redounds to the glory of God. 'In the beginning', as at the
end of the world process (according to Rev. 21.22), there is
no need of a temple made with hands; such things are need-
ful only as a result of man's fallen state. Nor in the original
creation was there need of sun or moon to give light: light,
which throughout the Bible symbolizes the revelation of
God's truth and glory, is created *before* the sun, on the first
'day', and thereby God's majesty is revealed to the angelic
hosts (cf. Job 38.7). How stupid was the old objection that
light was created three days before the sun was made! The
author is poetically telling us concerning the first creation
precisely the same thing as John the Seer tells us about the
New Creation, New Jerusalem: 'the city hath no need of
the sun . . . for the glory of God did lighten it' (Rev.
21.23). The whole world in God's original design was his
Temple, not in the sense that he could be confined within it
or was dependent upon it: the P school had learnt (and
indeed had taught) the lesson of the Exile that God was
infinitely greater than his Temple and was not destroyed
along with it. God transcends the universe which he has
made, just as his Presence is not confined within the Temple
on Mount Zion; nevertheless God is present to his works
which he sees to be good, and his glory is revealed in them
to the eyes which are illumined by his light. 'The heavens
declare the glory of God . . .' (Ps. 19, which may be read as
a commentary upon P's creation story).

Once we have imaginatively grasped the Priestly conception of all created things as ceaselessly fulfilling their
appointed 'liturgy' (service) to the greater glory of God, we
shall come to hear P's stylized refrains almost as liturgical
'responses'—antiphons in the great offering of praise and
thanksgiving that continually ascends from the creation to
the Creator. Each divine act of creation is introduced by

'And God said'; the refrain 'And it was so' occurs six
times; 'God saw that it was good', six times, leading to the
climax 'very good'; 'there was evening and there was morning' is the repeated refrain of each creative act; and there
are recurring phrases like 'after its kind'. These reflec-
tions prompt the question whether perhaps our P Creation
Story took shape in the liturgy of the Temple. It may quite
effectively be used in recital, the refrains being chanted
antiphonally by the choir or some part of the congregation;
and it is not improbable that it took its origin in this way.
We do not know; but it is clear that as a great Hymn of the
Creation it might be fittingly used when the people of God
are come together to sing their *Te Deum* in glad and solemn
commemoration of that day 'when the morning stars sang
together, and all the sons of God shouted for joy' (Job 38.7;
cf. Ps. 100).

1. In the beginning

The phrase means 'at the beginning, before the creation
of anything'. It is not used in any philosophical sense, for
the Hebrew mind did not speculate upon such questions as
the relation of time to eternity. The biblical writers everywhere are content to assert God's lordship over time (cf.
Ps. 90.4; II Pet. 3.8, etc.). They do not discuss whether
God is 'outside time', or what happened 'before time
began'. They conceive time as stretching in an endless succession backwards and forwards, and they treat of those
deep questions which pass man's understanding by means
of parable and poetic image. IN THE BEGINNING might almost
be read as 'once upon a time', provided that we do not
assume that what follows is 'merely' fairy-tale. The fact
here to be asserted is: IN THE BEGINNING GOD; this is the
fundamental certainty of revelation. The N.T. amplifies:
'In the beginning the creative Word of God, now made
known in Christ . . .' (John 1.1; Col. 1.16; Heb. 1.2; Rev.
3.14, etc.).

God

The word used is the ordinary Hebrew word for God, *Elohim*. It is plural in form, but it is not therefore to be regarded as merely a survival from an earlier polytheistic stage of religious development. It represents a deep biblical insight: God is not, and never was, a lonely God. There is personality in God, and a person could not exist alone. The Bible could never have used the name for God which we find in Greek philosophers and mystics like Plotinus, 'the Alone'. God did not need to create a world in order to possess an object for his love. We cannot, of course, imagine what God is like in the transcendence of his being, or how he can exist apart from the world as a society of love. The O.T. writers convey the richly personal or societal nature of God's being by their imagery of God surrounded by his heavenly court, his angels, spirits, ministers—the 'sons of God'. We have here a poetical conception, which is spoilt if taken in a woodenly literalistic way (cf. for examples, I Kings 22.19-22; Job 1.6-12; Isa. 6.1-8). God is the supreme and 'only' God, but he is not 'alone'. Hence the use of the plural in several passages (e.g., Gen. 1.26, 'Let *us* make man'; 3.22; 11.7, etc.). The Christian Fathers and the older commentators regarded such passages as adumbrations of the Christian doctrine of the Trinity. Of course the O.T. writers had no such conception in mind; but yet they were in their own way insisting upon that truth which the doctrine of the Trinity teaches—that a 'unitarian' or lonely God is not the God of the historic biblical revelation.

created

Whether the word (*bara'*) means creation *ex nihilo* in an absolute sense may be left to the specialists to decide. But it is clear that something very near that is intended. The word is used only of God and is frequent in the Second Isaiah (Isa. 40.26, 28; 42.5; 45.7, 12, 18). It implies something utterly beyond human imitation or comprehension, for the work of creation is essentially miraculous.

the heaven and the earth

That is, the whole universe. The first verse constitutes a summary of the story that is unfolded in the rest of the chapter.

2. waste and void

'Without shape and desolate.' It is not implied that this undifferentiated watery substance was what the Creator had to go to work upon, but that the first stage of creation carried the process only thus far. Everything as yet was in a state of chaos (*tohu wa-bohu*), but the work will continue: God did not create the earth to be a *tohu* but to be inhabited (Isa. 45.18).

darkness was upon the face of the deep

We must not import into the biblical symbolism any modern scientific notions, such as that darkness is only a negative quality, a mere privation of light. In the Bible darkness is positive; it is as real as light; it signifies mystery (and, in some contexts, evil). God, considered as transcendent and ineffable, is said to dwell in thick darkness (I Kings 8.12; Ps. 18.11; 97.2, etc.). There is thus a real dualism of light and darkness in the Bible (cf. esp. the Fourth Gospel), but it is not an ultimate dualism, since God is the Creator and Lord of the darkness as well as of the light (Ps. 104.20; Isa. 45.7). Therefore darkness is no embarrassment to him as it is to us (Ps. 139.11f.). In the biblical symbolism God's utter sovereignty is expressed by proclaiming his lordship over the darkness and over 'the deep', i.e., the waste of waters: the sea was always a terrifying element to the Hebrews. In the primitive cosmogony of the Semites the deep (Heb. *tehom*) seems to have been associated with the beginnings of things (cf. the Babylonian *Tiamat*); it sym-

bolizes the dark and mysterious unknown. God's power is
nowhere more dramatically described than in those O.T.
passages in which he is portrayed as in control of the deep
and of the waves and storms of the sea (e.g., Ps. 33.7f.; 93;
107.23-32). It is against this background that we must
understand the Sea-Miracles of Jesus, the Stilling of the
Storm and the Walking on the Sea (cf. Mark 4.41: 'Who
then is this, that even the wind and the sea obey him?'; also
Mark 6.51); so, too, must we understand the symbolism of
(e.g.) the 'darkness over all the earth' at the Crucifixion.

the spirit of God moved

Ruach is wind, breath or spirit; it denotes the vital
element in man (cp. 'gave up the spirit', Mark 15.39), and
when used of God it might refer to his life-giving power
(cf. 2.7 and note below). But here the expression is hardly
more than a Hebrew idiom meaning 'a very strong wind',
and it can scarcely be used to support a doctrine of the
Creator Spirit. Nevertheless, whatever the expression 'spirit
of God' might mean as a Hebrew idiom taken by itself, the
sentence as a whole suggests a remarkable poetic image of
God hovering or brooding (RV marg.) like a mother-bird
over the new-born world (cf. Deut. 32.11, the only other use
in the O.T. of the word here translated 'moved').

3. And God said, Let there be . . .

Here we meet with the O.T. doctrine of the creative *word*
of God. The biblical writers seek to go beyond the
anthropomorphic conception of God as making the world
with his hands out of some pre-existent material, as a potter
makes vessels of clay—though on occasion they are not at
all averse to anthropomorphism. They do this by means of
the conception of creation by *fiat* (LET THERE BE); God calls
the world into existence simply by speaking a word: 'God
said, Let there be . . . and it was so.' Thus the absolute
power and creativity of God are most effectively suggested;

God utters his word and his will is immediately accomplished (cf. Ps. 33.6, 9: 'By the word of Jehovah were the heavens made, and all the host of them (i.e., the stars) by the breath (*ruach*) of his mouth. . . . For he spake and it was done; he commanded and it stood fast'). God not only creates the world with his word; he also orders it and controls the processes of nature with his word, and with his word he makes known his will to men (cf. Ps. 147.18f.: 'He sendeth out his word and melteth them (*sc.* the ice and snow) . . . he showeth his word unto Jacob, his statutes and his judgments unto Israel'). God's word spoken by his prophets has an irresistible self-fulfilling efficacy; it must inevitably accomplish that to which it is sent (Isa. 55.11). In the Gospels attention is called to this same power of the word which is spoken by our Lord; he casts out the demons with a word (Matt. 8.16); he need 'speak the word only' and a sick man is healed (Matt. 8.8; cp. Ps. 107.20); he commands even the wind and the sea, and they obey him (Mark 4.41). The N.T. depicts Christ as calling into existence the New People of God and as thus achieving the New Creation (cf. II Cor. 5.17; Gal. 6.15), the 'earnest' of the New Heaven and New Earth. The Fourth Gospel brings the biblical thinking about the creative word of God to its climax in its teaching that Christ is the Incarnate Word of God: the very word which was God's instrument in the first creation, without which was not anything made that was made, became flesh and dwelt among men, so that his disciples beheld his glory, full of grace and truth (John 1.1-14).

light

In the biblical symbolism light is a recurring and pregnant image. It bears a wide and varied range of meanings. It often signifies the presence of God himself (cf. I John 1.5, 'God is light'), or the favour of God's presence (cf. 'the light of thy countenance', Ps. 89.15; 90.8, etc.), or the dwelling-place of God (I Tim. 6.16, etc.). It denotes

the character of God, in accordance with which his people
must walk (Ps. 89.15; Rom. 13.12f.; I John 1.5ff.). Since
the only bright light that was known in the ancient world
was the light of the sun, 'light' is often used (as here)
synonymously with 'day' (cf. I Thess. 5.5). Sometimes light
symbolizes prosperity and darkness adversity; often light
represents moral probity and darkness evil deeds (John
3.16-21; cp. 13.30). Above all, it should be noted that where-
ever 'light' is mentioned in the Bible in a symbolic sense
the idea of revelation is not far away; light is the frequent
and obvious symbol of the unveiling of the truth (cf. Eph.
5.13). Hence the Fourth Gospel speaks of Christ as 'the
light of the world' (John 11.9; cf. 12.35f.); the coming of
Christ was the coming of the 'true light' (John 1.4f., 9).
Perhaps the culminating biblical word on the theme of light
belongs not to St. John but to St. Paul: 'It is God who
said, Light shall shine out of darkness, who shined in our
hearts, to give the illumination of the knowledge of the glory
of God in the face of Jesus Christ' (II Cor. 4.6). In the first
part of this verse St. Paul is clearly alluding to Gen. 1.3. As
the word of God, active in the work of creation, is incarnate
in Jesus Christ, so the light which illumined the first day of
creation is revealed as the glory of God in the face of Jesus
Christ. And as it was in the beginning, so it shall be at the
end: the day of the Lord will be the day of light, when the
secrets of all hearts shall be disclosed, the day of revelation,
of unveiling: in the end, as at the beginning, the light
exists apart from the sun and moon and stars, because
in the biblical poetic imagery it is the light of God's own
presence.

4. God saw . . . that it was good

This recurrent phrase emphasizes the joy and satisfaction
of the Creator in his work. It also expresses the biblical
insight that the world *as made by God* was in no way defec-
tive or marred by evil.

5. there was evening and there was morning

In the Hebrew reckoning the day begins and ends not as with us at midnight, but at sunset. Hence the Bible often speaks of 'night and day' whereas we should say 'day and night' (e.g. Mark 4.27). (A survival of this biblical way of reckoning is seen in the Christian Church in the liturgical practice of saying the Collect of the Day for the first time at Evensong on what we should call the day before it.) It is hardly necessary to add that the 'days' of creation are to be understood as poetic symbols and not as definite periods of time, whether of twenty-four hours, or of a thousand years, or of a geological epoch.

6. a firmament in the midst of the waters

The ancients believed that the sky was *something solid* (which is what FIRMAMENT literally means). It was like a great inverted basin, beaten out as from metal, and quite impenetrable except through doors. The stars were fixed in the solid sky like jewels. Above the sky was water, and rain came down through doors or sluices from the waters above the firmament (cf. Ps. 148.4). Above these waters was the abode of God himself. The firmament rested upon pillars at the ends or corners of the earth. For glimpses of the primitive cosmology in the O.T. see (e.g.) Job 26.11; 37.18; Ps. 104.3, 13; Amos 9.6. The calling into being of the sky, which divides the upper from the lower waters on which the earth floats or in which it stands on pillars, is the work of the second day of creation.

9-13. On the third day of creation the earth is separated off from the waters below the firmament and the vegetable kingdom is created. The Hebrews conceived of the earth as a relatively small area of land floating on (or standing in) the abyss of waters; cf. Exod. 20.4; Ps. 24.2; 136.6, and many other such passages. There is a magnificent description of the third day of creation in Ps. 104.6-8; cf. also Job 38.8-11.

14-19. On the fourth day of creation the sun, moon and stars are made. They are thought of as fastened on to the firmament, in which they have been assigned regular tracks. These LIGHTS give the earth its necessary physical illumination—perhaps the making of the firmament had cut off the regions beneath it from the source of the divine light—but they are distinct from and inferior to the light which had appeared on the first day, a light which was much more than merely physical. Three points should be noted in this section. First, there is here expressed a deep sense of the regularity of the heavenly bodies in their appointed courses. Their regularity is, however, liturgical, like that of the priests in their courses at the Temple; it is not that of Kepler, who aspired to turn the universe into clockwork, 'believing that this was the highest thing he could do to glorify God' (H. Butterfield, *Origins of Modern Science*, 1950, p. 59). But though P's universe is very different in conception from the mathematical orderliness of Newton's 'clean and empty heavens', it too proclaims its 'great Original', for P unquestionably shares the Psalmist's conviction that 'the heavens declare the glory of God, and the firmament sheweth his handywork' (Ps. 19.1). Secondly, there is also here the clear understanding, so germane to the biblical outlook, that God is the Lord of time; times and seasons, days and years, have been predetermined by God when he made the heavens. This truth would seem of particular importance to the P school with their special interest in the liturgical calendar. And thirdly, we should note that in view of the unquestioned universal belief of the ancient world (outside Israel) that the heavenly bodies are living, divine beings (even Aristotle believed this), P's silent rejection of this view is very impressive. The worship of 'the host of heaven' (i.e. the stars) was a commonplace of pagan religion; but the men of the Bible, because they know the Creator, are not addicted to the worship of the creature (cf. Deut. 4.19; Jer. 44.17ff.; Wisd. 13.2, etc.).

20-23. On the fifth day of creation are made the birds and the fishes—all the creatures of the air and the sea. They receive the divine approval and blessing; they are to BE FRUITFUL AND MULTIPLY (one of P's characteristic phrases), that they too may perform their appointed function in the created order, the liturgy of adoration of what we should call the world of nature.

24-31. The sixth day of creation sees the climax and completion of the immense divine work. First comes the creation of the beasts and reptiles, which is followed by the crowning event of the whole process, the creation of man. Man is conceived of as the high-priest of the order of creation; the world that God has made is a theocracy (like the Jewish nation after the Exile), ruled over by a high-priest who is God's vicegerent, to whom is committed the dominion over all created things.

26. Let us make man

For the plural LET US see note on 1.1, *God* (*Elohim*). The word for MAN (*adam*) here is collective—' mankind '. P does not speak of the creation of a pair of individuals, *a* man and *a* woman (as does J), but of the human species; in the same way he has already spoken of the creation of fish, beasts, etc., AFTER THEIR KIND, not as individual fishes, beasts, etc. It is mankind as such that is made in God's image.

in our image, after our likeness

The Bible makes it clear that there is an essential difference between man and even the highest mammals. It is well aware that man shares with the animals certain characteristics, chief of which is his mortality (cf. Ps. 49.12: ' Man is like the beasts that perish '; also Ps. 144.3f.). But he differs from the animals in that God ' visits ' him, i.e., holds converse with him (Ps. 8.4): there is that in man which the animals do not possess, namely, man's responsibility

before God, the fact that he can *answer* God's address, hear
his law and make (or withhold) his conscious and deliberate
response. There is that in man which is capable of respond-
ing to the divine Word; man is akin to God in this respect
at least, that he hears God's Word: as we say, 'like speaks
to like'. This is what is meant by P when he says that man
is made in God's image and implies that no other creature
is so made. All the rest of the creation obeys God's will
without conscious volition: the stars in their courses
mechanically complete their appointed liturgy; even the
animals fulfil by instinct the law of their creation. To man
alone is given the responsibility of conscious choice; man
alone of all created things is free to disobey the Creator's
will. Thus it is that man alone is conscious of his responsibility before God, is aware that he stands in the presence
and under the judgment of God. Some theologians have
suggested that the image of God was lost by man at the Fall
(i.e., as the result of sin), but this is not the biblical view.
P teaches that the divine image in man is transmitted from
generation to generation, even after sin has entered the
world (Gen. 5.1, 3; 9.6). The biblical position can best be
summarized by saying that the divine image is defaced but
not obliterated at the Fall (or by man's sin). Sometimes,
too, theologians from the time of Irenaeus (died *c*. A.D. 202)
onwards have attempted to build theories on a supposed
distinction between IMAGE and LIKENESS. But no such distinction exists in P's intention; we have here a straight-
forward case of Hebrew parallelism, in which a second
phrase repeats the meaning of the phrase that has gone
before. The words mean: 'in God's image, that is to say,
in his likeness' (so W. Eichrodt).

let them have dominion

It has become the fashion in certain quarters to assert
that God's likeness in man is most clearly perceived in the
fact that man shares in God's creativity; we hear much

about man's 'creative' powers, as artists, craftsmen, scientists, and so on. The *imago Dei* is made to consist in man's capacity for creative activity. This is not what the Bible teaches. It is clear that P thinks of the likeness of God in man as manifest in man's sharing in the Creator's *dominium* over the rest of the created order, especially over the animal world. This essentially biblical teaching is most clearly enunciated in Ps. 8.5-8:

> Thou hast made him but little lower than *Elohim* (see on 1.1),
> And crownest him with glory and honour.
> Thou madest him to have dominion over the works of thy hands;
> Thou hast put all things under his feet:
> All sheep and oxen,
> Yea, and the beasts of the field;
> The fowl of the air, and the fish of the sea,
> Whatsoever passeth through the paths of the seas.

Clearly God's image in man is not obliterated. May we not see (e.g.) in the marvels of modern science, and in the astounding dominion over the world of nature which man has achieved thereby, a partial fulfilment of the divine intention in the creation that man should 'subdue' the earth (v. 28)? But man must remember that he is lord of creation and ruler of nature not in his own right or to work his own will; he is God's vicegerent, charged with the working of God's will, responsible to God for his stewardship. Otherwise his science and industry will bring not a blessing but a curse; they will make of the earth not a paradise but a dust-bowl or a Hiroshima. When we survey human history and review the sad spectacle of man's age-long effort to subdue the earth to his own ends and not to God's glory, we understand that the divine image in man is indeed defaced. The doctrine of the *imago Dei* is closely connected

with the doctrine of the *dominium*; the former shows us
what man *is*, the latter shows us what is his function. When
the image is obscured, then the dominion is impaired; when
the image is restored, the dominion is fulfilled. The N.T.
shows how in Christ the true divine image in man has by
God's grace been restored; we see in Christ what we cannot
see in fallen humanity, the perfect image of the invisible
God, as it had been first brought forth (*prototokos*) before
all creation (Col. 1.15; cf. Heb. 1.3). It is not in fallen mankind that the promise contained in Gen. 1.26-28 will be
fulfilled; it will be fulfilled in the redeemed humanity of the
Last Adam, the Church of Christ: 'whom he foreknew, he
also foreordained to be conformed to the image of his Son'
(Rom. 8.29): 'we are transformed into the same image,
from glory to glory' (II Cor. 3.18): our 'new man' is being
'renewed unto knowledge after the image of him that
created him' (Col. 3.10). Cf. also Heb. 2.5-10.

27. And God created man

The unique significance of the creation of man is
emphasized by the way in which the weighty word 'create'
(*bara'*, see on 1.1), not hitherto employed except in the summary in v. 1, is now used three times in rapid succession.

male and female created he them

By insisting that woman is not created after man (contrast
J, Gen. 2.18ff.) but along with him, P teaches that men and
women are equally important and are complementary to
each other in God's design. In the Creator's original intention there was no superiority of the man, just as in the 'new
creation' in which the original intention is re-established
there is no distinction of male and female in Christ (Gal.
3.28)—whatever distinctions there may be between the Fall
and the Restoration of all things in Christ. It is also explicit
in P's teaching that the division of mankind into two sexes
is not a result of the Fall; it is part of God's original plan,

which he saw was 'very good'. On this insight our Lord based his teaching concerning the institution of marriage (Mark 10.6). Despite the fact that J in his account of the creation places the creation of woman after that of man, there is, as we shall see, no fundamental divergence of outlook between his teaching and that of P; see notes on the section 2.18-25.

28. And God blessed them

In its context this phrase sounds like a blessing given at a marriage: man and woman are blessed and are to be fruitful and multiply. Thus there is no suggestion that child-bearing as such is a punishment for sin; procreation belongs to the world which God saw to be 'very good'. In the strength of the divine blessing the human race goes forward to its task of replenishing and subduing the earth. As he blesses, God makes provision for the sustenance both of human and of animal life (vv. 29f.). This provision is of a purely vegetarian diet; in the creation as God planned it there was to be no 'struggle for existence'. It is thus implied that 'nature red in tooth and claw' is in some way (we are not told how) a result of the entry of sin into the world. Cf. 6.21 and 9.3 with notes *ad loc.*

30. wherein there is life

Heb., literally 'a living soul' (RV margin). See note on this phrase under 2.7.

31. behold, it was very good

There is a significant variation of the formula now that the climax of the creation has been achieved: God sees the finished work, and he sees it to be *very* good.

2.1-4a. On the seventh day the Creator rests from his work.

After the Exile, perhaps at the very time when the traditional P material was being collected and written down, the Sabbath was becoming more and more markedly a distinguishing feature of the life of the Jews (cf. Neh. 10.31; 13.15-22). An attempt was being made rigorously to enforce the law of total abstention from any kind of work on the Sabbath; and at a still later period this law was kept by devout Jews with fanatical enthusiasm (cf. I Mac. 2.34-41 and the evidence of the Gospels). It is clear that the Sabbath was not so observed in pre-Exilic times (see, e.g., II Kings 4.22f.). By the days of Jeremiah and Ezekiel, however, the keeping of the Sabbath had become a recognized sign of devotion to Jehovah (cf. Jer. 17.21-27, but perhaps this passage is a later addition; Ezek. 20.12-20; cf. Isa. 56.2-8; 58.13f.). Various explanations of the meaning of the Sabbath are given in the different strata of the O.T. In the prophetic passages above listed it is a ' sign ' between Jehovah and the People of the inviolability of the covenant between them; in Deut. 5.12-15 it is a memorial of the deliverance from Egypt; in P it is a memorial of the finished work of the creation and of the Creator's rest (Gen. 2.1ff.; Exod. 20.11; 31.17). The question of the actual origins of the Sabbath amongst the early Israelites in far-off nomadic days is very obscure and complicated (see N. H. Snaith, *The Jewish New Year Festival*, pp. 103ff.); perhaps it was a lunar festival (cf. II Chron. 2.4)—the week of seven days is, of course, based upon the lunar month and the Sabbath would thus correspond to the quarterly phases of the moon. Nomads travel by night (for safety in moving their herds), and the moon is more important in their lives than the sun, since they do not depend upon the latter as settled agriculturalist peoples do. P's explanation is indubitably aetiological, that is, it discovers a developed religious motive to sanction or re-interpret a custom which had its origins in a much more primitive (and probably to later eyes somewhat disreputable) view of things.

(b) THE SECOND CREATION STORY
2.4b-25; J

In the Introduction we have already indicated the general
character of the J narrative. It is unnecessary here to point
out the complete change in thought and style which is apparent in the middle of 2.4. P's 'liturgical' outlook, together
with his stylized expressions and repeated formulæ, now gives
place to a beautiful idyll, childlike in its simplicity yet profound in its insight. We should notice that the whole section
2.4b-3.24 is a unity, not divided in the author's mind (as
we usually treat it for the sake of convenience) into *two*
separate parables of Creation and Fall.

J's teaching about the creation of the world by God and
man's place in the creation is basically the same as P's, but
it is quite differently conveyed. J's creation story is more
truly a parable than P's, which is not so much a parable as
a solemn liturgical recital. For example, P speaks of the
creation of *mankind*, and he does not personify 'man' under
the form of a single individual; in P 'adam' is a generic
noun. But J on the other hand personifies mankind under
the figure of a single man (and his wife); in J 'Adam' becomes a proper name. But it is only the form of the teaching in which J differs from P; J's Adam is a poetic
personification rather than an actual, historical individual.
To imagine that J intended his parable to be taken *à pied de
la lettre* is a purely gratuitous assumption, almost certainly
false.

The differences between P's and J's accounts of the
creation need not perplex us, once we have grasped how the
two stories had completely different origins, and when we
have understood the poetic and non-literalistic nature of
each story. The principal material difference between the
two stories lies in the order of the incidents in the creation.
In P man is created last, after vegetation, birds, fishes and
beasts, and woman is created at the same time as man. In

J man is created first, then the trees, then the beasts and birds, and finally woman. In his story J includes insights which P does not contain (and *vice versa*), but the principal meaning of the two stories is the same. P teaches that man is the crown and high-priest of the created order by placing man's creation last; J teaches that man is the chief of all created things by placing his creation first and by the whole way in which he tells his story. But, as we shall see, he is not intending to suggest that woman is an inferior work of the Creator by placing her creation last: it is simply that the shape of the story demands this particular order, and the purpose of it is the very point which P has made—that woman is complementary to man, who is incomplete and ' alone ' without her.

4b. in the day that

The word DAY does not here mean a precise period of twelve or twenty-four hours; the expression in Hebrew idiom means ' at the time when '.

the LORD God

LORD, i.e., Jahweh, the name revealed by God to Moses (Exod. 6.2f.), is used from the beginning by the J writer(s): see Introduction. Jahweh (or Jehovah) is the name by which Israel knows God as *their* God. The expression THE LORD GOD (*Jahweh Elohim*) is in the O.T. almost peculiar to this section (Gen. 2.4b–3.25), and some critics have thought that *Elohim* has been added by the editor to identify Jahweh with the ' God ' of Chap. I. In the RV ' LORD ' is printed thus in capitals to indicate that the Hebrew is *Jehovah*; see RV marginal note to this verse.

made earth and heaven

J does not use P's word *bara'*, create. His language is throughout more anthropomorphic. God CAUSED IT TO RAIN, FORMED MAN OF THE DUST, PLANTED A GARDEN, took one of

Adam's ribs, and so on.   Such language is the language of parable, and it is not to be supposed that J literally conceives of God as working with his hands or possessing a body like a man's.   Such childishness would be incompatible with the simple, majestic and indeed transcendent conception implicit in the phrase, ' Jahweh God made earth and heaven ', and with the whole conception of God in J.

5. the LORD God had not caused it to rain
In contrast to P's account the earth is originally very dry in J's narrative.

6. a mist—or, possibly, a flood.

7. The LORD God formed man of the dust
J expresses here in a wonderful poetic figure an essentially biblical insight, namely, the fact of man's creatureliness. FORMED is ' moulded ', as a potter moulds clay.   Man is no divine or semi-divine being, who may claim equality with God (cf. 3.5) in virtue of his ' spiritual ' nature : he is but ' living dust '.   St. Paul has this verse in mind when he writes, ' The first man is of the earth, earthy ' (I Cor. 15.47) : our human nature, until it is redeemed in Christ, is ter-restrial, earth-bound, corruptible.

the breath of life
BREATH and LIFE in animals are, if not synonymous, at least co-existent ; dead bodies do not breathe.   Here in another poetic image J asserts that life comes from God, that God is the source of life.   It is by a miracle that God creates animated dust ; modern science has done nothing to diminish the mystery of life or to suggest for it any other source than God.   The bestowal of the divine breath upon man is probably J's equivalent of P's ' image of God '.   J does not say that God breathed his breath into the animals.

a living soul

SOUL does not here mean 'spiritual element' (as in the expression 'our immortal souls'); it simply means life—animal life. The phrase merely means: 'man became a living being', or 'man began to live'. The Hebrews held no high-falutin' notions about man's spirituality; they did not (as the Greeks did) think of his 'soul' as the higher part of him, imprisoned in his vile body, or as a kind of indestructible soul-substance. For the biblical writers man is a living body (rather than a living soul in the modern sense of the word), and his body, being God-created, is not vile. It was an essential part of him, the means of self-expression, not his 'prison' or 'tomb'. Hence it was natural for St. Paul to speak of the resurrection of the body—that is, of man as a total personality: not a ghost or yet a purely 'spiritual' being, but having the essential means of self-expression, communication, recognizability, and all the other things which are included in the full idea of what we to-day would call 'personality'.

8. the LORD God planted a garden

GARDEN, more correctly a park (LXX, 'paradise', originally a Persian word denoting a nobleman's park). The park is situated 'eastward', i.e., presumably east of Canaan, out in the direction of Babylonia, the oldest civilization that the Hebrews knew.

Eden

The word means 'delight', 'enchantment', 'pleasure'. But perhaps it is intended only as a proper name, a place-name. Some have connected it with the Babylonian *edinu*, a plain. Attempts to locate a geographical site of EDEN are as foolish as trying to identify the spot on the road from Jerusalem to Jericho where the traveller was attacked by robbers in the parable of the Good Samaritan. To the Hebrew mind the phrase would suggest 'garden of delight'

(cf. the Christian symbol ' paradise '). Man was created by
God to dwell in ' paradise ', that is, in blessed fellowship ⚹
with himself and in the enjoyment of the manifold riches of
his creation. But man was not created for idleness; he has
his proper function to perform in the created order. Eden
is not to be for him a ' lotus-eater's paradise '. In J's parable
man is put into the garden TO DRESS IT AND TO KEEP IT
(v. 15), just as in P he is created to exercise dominion under
God over the created order. It is not suggested that the
trees in the garden (v. 9), which are pleasant to behold and
good for food, will sustain man's life if he does not expend
upon them due care and toil. We may note in v. 9 how J
stresses in his own way the excellence of God's original
creation, an insight which corresponds to P's GOD SAW THAT
IT WAS GOOD.

9. the tree of life

Possibly this image is suggested by the primitive legends
of magic trees, the fruit of which was a medicine of im-
mortality. But J transmutes the idea far beyond the region
of legend and magic. The tree of life represents man's unbroken communion with God. Such communion is proof
against mortality. But man by his sin is excluded from
unbroken communion with the holy God, as the parable
goes on to show (3.22-24). The biblical writers look forward
to its restoration. Thus, Ezekiel, using this same symbol of
the tree of life, envisages the presence of such trees, watered
by the river of life which flows out from the Temple in his
idealized Jerusalem (Ezek. 47.12). What the prophet has
foreseen in his vision has been eschatologically realized in
Jesus Christ—so the author of the Book of Revelation
teaches: communion with God is made possible again
through Christ. Therefore the seer, using the same symbolism, depicts the tree of life standing in the street of the
New Jerusalem by the ' pure river of the water of life ': ' and
the leaves of the tree were for the healing of the nations '

(Rev. 22.2). Elsewhere he describes the tree of life as the
reward of faithfulness (Rev. 2.7; 22.14). The description of
wisdom as a tree of life in Prov. 3.18 is an independent
metaphor which hardly belongs to this cycle of ideas (cf. also
Prov. 11.30). These are the only occurrences of the expression in the Bible. It may be that the New Testament references to the cross as a ' tree ' (Acts 5.30; 10.39; 13.29; Gal.
3.13; I Pet. 2.24) are intended to suggest the idea of the
cross of Christ as THE TREE OF LIFE; biblical images frequently overlap one another. But the primary reference of
these expressions is undoubtedly to Deut. 21.23, ' Cursed is
every one that hangeth on a tree ', cited by St. Paul in Gal.
3.13.

the tree of the knowledge of good and evil

This particular symbol occurs in the Bible only in this
parable (Gen. 2.4–3.24). Hence the interpretation of it is of
peculiar difficulty. This (not THE TREE OF LIFE) is the tree
whose fruit is forbidden to man (v. 17, etc.). In Hebrew
usage the expression ' good and evil ' does not necessarily
imply moral good and evil; it means ' everything, good and
bad '. Thus, the expression KNOWLEDGE OF GOOD AND EVIL
is synonymous with ' all knowledge '. The notion, often
encountered, that it has some special connection with sexual
knowledge is a complete mistake. But KNOWLEDGE must
be understood in a biblical, not a Greek, sense; it is knowledge gained by participating actively in the affairs of life—
not ' academic ' or theoretical knowledge, but what in our
jargon of to-day we might call ' existential ' knowledge. A
more usual English word would be ' experience '. Thus,
THE TREE OF THE KNOWLEDGE OF GOOD AND EVIL is a symbol
denoting ' human experience in its entirety '. The significance of this symbol will be made clearer under verse 2.17
and in the sequel.

10-14. These verses interrupt the proper development of the parable and are not strictly germane to it. They introduce actual geographical features into what is otherwise a purely symbolic story. In that part of the world known to the O.T. writers rivers are the great source of fertility; and agriculture—and indeed civilization itself—flourishes only in the valleys which they irrigate. Thus the notion of a 'river of life' or of 'living waters' would arise quite naturally (cf. Ezek. 47; Rev. 22, etc.), and it becomes a well-marked feature of the biblical symbolism in its various forms. In this passage the fructifying power of the great rivers known to J is attributed to the fact that they take their origin from the RIVER that WENT OUT OF EDEN: even the blessings of nature are ultimately derived from the grace of God in the creation. PISHON (not elsewhere mentioned in O.T.) may be the far-away Indus, but the mention of gold and precious stones suggests somewhere in Arabia (?*Havilah*), famous for these things. GIHON has been traditionally identified with the Nile (but why should the Nile not be given its well-known name?); CUSH is Ethiopia. HIDDEKEL is the Tigris. IN FRONT OF means 'east of' Assyria. EUPHRATES needed no description. These four great rivers (and by inference the civilizations in their valleys) are thought of—probably poetically—as taking their rise in the river that flowed out from Eden, the source of all life.

15. to dress it and to keep it

This verse should dispose entirely of the notion that the Bible teaches that work is a curse, a punishment inflicted by God on account of man's sin (cf. 3.17-19). Man was created by God to be a worker; he is assigned his work *before* he transgresses. See also on 2.8.

17. thou shalt surely die

If, as we have seen (on 2.9), THE TREE OF THE KNOWLEDGE OF GOOD AND EVIL symbolizes human experience in its entirety, then these words mean that to participate in human experience involves mortality. There is deep insight here. Human experience, *qua* human, necessarily involves freedom, for man is not an automaton. Human life *is* choice, decision; and choice involves the inevitability of choosing right *and* wrong. Human experience is inevitably sinful experience, and sin has its consequence in death. This is the outlook of the Bible in every part. When ' Adam ' becomes truly human, he becomes thereby mortal. See further under 3.5.

18. It is not good that man should be alone
Another deep insight is here expressed. Man was made for fellowship not for isolation. To isolate oneself from one's fellows perverts human nature as divinely created. True human experience cannot begin until the self has an ' other ' over against whom it stands; lonely existence is not fully human existence. The parable delightfully represents the creation of the animals as an experiment in providing man with ' others ' with whom he may enter into fully personal relationships and through fellowship with whom he may attain his true human stature. The experiment, of course, does not succeed; it is only through fellowship with his equals that man can truly realize himself.

an help meet for him
lit. ' a help answering to him ' (RV margin): one who ' answers ', one with whom the self can enter into *responsible* relations. (Note that the word ' helpmeet ' or ' helpmate ', derived from this text, is a solecism based on misunderstanding; the narrative does not suggest that woman was created as a kind of ' first mate ' under man as the skipper!)

19. The LORD God formed every beast
Like man, the animals are moulded out of the ground. Jehovah is not said to breathe into their nostrils the breath of

life, but it is doubtful whether J regarded this as specially
significant; for the Hebrew mind animals, like men, are
'living souls' (i.e., living bodies: see on v. 7). The difference for the biblical writers between men and the animals
is not that men have 'souls' and animals have not, but that
God 'visits' or speaks to men, and that they enter into
personal relationships with him.

20. And the man gave names

Again there is profound significance beneath the charming
fable of the naming of the animals. Names were very important in Hebrew thought; a name represented a person's
character, his real self. To know a man's name was to
know the man himself, to enter as it were into his personal
being. Hence the significance of the fact that God had
revealed his name (Jehovah) to Israel and to Israel alone
(Exod. 6.2f.; cf. Gen. 32.27-29); hence Israel was privileged
to enter into personal relationship with God and to share
in the divine life. We do not give their names to the people
whom we encounter; we meet them and learn their names.
To give a name to someone implies authority over him (as
when our Lord surnames Simon with his new character,
Peter, the Rock). Man names the animals; that is, he
assigns to them their status and character—he defines and
determines their being. This is J's equivalent of P's asser-
tion that man has been given the dominion OVER EVERY
LIVING THING (1.28).

21. a deep sleep

Needless to say, there is no suggestion here of administer-
ing an anæsthetic while an operation is performed! Behind
this element of the parable there doubtless lies the primitive
notion that man must not behold the miracles of God, which
are secret processes known to God alone. But the idea of
mystery that is here suggested is wholly appropriate and
right: here is the mystery of God's creation of mankind in

two sexes—a fact which we cannot explain, but one which we must accept with reverence and thankfulness.

22. and the rib . . . made he a woman

In this wonderful allegory God does not make woman out of different ground from Adam's, as he makes the animals; he makes her out of a part of Adam's body, significantly his side. A woman's place is at the side of the man: to be his companion, his fitting ' help ', the sharer in all his life. The high esteem in which the Bible holds women (unlike many other ancient peoples) is fittingly represented by this symbolism: woman stands by man's side—not behind him or before him. The wives of the Patriarchs in the later Genesis stories, who stand so loyally by the side of their husbands, represent faithfully the Hebrew ideal of womanhood. But the symbolism indicates also the woman's dependence upon the man; she has no independent existence apart from him, just as he has no fitting completion apart from her. By the act of creating woman the divine work of creating man is completed; thus J expresses the same fundamental insight as does P in his account of the simultaneous creation of man and woman (1.27).

and brought her unto the man

As in P (1.28) the fundamental idea of marriage as a divine institution is here present: God himself ' gives away ' the woman at the nuptials of the human race.

23. Woman, because she was taken out of man

We are fortunate in the fact that the English language reproduces in the words MAN, WOMAN, the assonance of the Hebrew *Ish, Isshah* (see RV margin). The fact that Adam names the woman implies his authority over her (see on v. 20). This is an essentially biblical point of view: ' the husband is the head of the wife ' (Eph. 5.23); ' the head of the woman is the man ' (I Cor. 11.3), etc. Many modern

folk regard such teaching as intolerable, because it con-
tradicts the so-called 'equality of the sexes'. But the point
of view of the Bible is throughout hierarchical, not
equalitarian: in the wonderful order of creation each part
has its own proper place and function. To grasp at
'equality' with everyone and everything is, from the biblical
point of view, the 'sin of Adam', i.e., pride. In an age in
which everyone grasps at 'equality' and no one is willing
to take the form of a servant, the biblical teaching is bound
to give offence. But we must insist that false and sentimental
notions of the equality of the sexes do not exalt but dis-
honour womanhood, which has its own distinctive excellence
—an excellence that is different from the man's. The amazing insight of the J writer is seen in his recognition that it
is sin (pride, grasping at equality) which puts the sting into
the acceptance of one's proper place in God's created order:
the irksomeness of the man's 'rule' is the result of the Fall
(see 3.16). It is only in the 'new creation' of Christ that
the effects of the Fall are done away: in Christ 'there is
neither male nor female, for ye are all one man in Christ
Jesus' (Gal. 3.28). In Christian marriage the true relation
of the man and the woman is restored (read Eph. 5.22-33);
so rich and wonderful is it that the relationship between
husband and wife becomes the very antitype of the relation
between Christ and his Church.

24. Therefore shall a man leave . . . one flesh

Happily for us the commentary upon this verse is provided
by the authority of our Lord himself (Mark 10.7ff.). Man
and wife 'are no more twain, but one flesh'. God's intention in the creation was that the completed unit of mankind,
the unity husband-wife, should be indissoluble and life-long.
Moses, because of the hardness of men's hearts, had had to
modify the Creator's intention and to permit divorce for
certain causes. But now that the age of the Law was over
and the New Age of the Reign (Kingdom) of God had begun,

God's intention in making man in two sexes was to be fulfilled: ' what God hath joined together, let not man put asunder '.   How truly astonishing it is that J's insight should thus be vindicated as the final truth of the relation of the sexes by our Lord himself!   It is implied that monogamous marriage is grounded in the very order of things as appointed by the Creator; marriage, that is to say, is not a man-made convention, or a social arrangement which is relevant only in certain stages of social evolution or at the convenience of the contracting parties.   It is a part of the natural order, and nothing but misery and unrest will follow if this divinely ordained natural law is transgressed.

25. Naked . . . and . . . not ashamed

When man and wife belong utterly and unselfishly to each other there is no need of shame.   Yet, paradoxically, in our ' fallen ' world shame—modesty, reticence—is a virtue.

II

THE FALL
3.1-24; J

We are accustomed to divide chapter 2 from chapter 3 and to speak of the J stories of Creation and Fall. But it is important to remember that Gen. 2.4b–3.24 is one complete and continuous parable, an artistic unity.

1. the serpent

In the lore of the Semitic races the SERPENT is proverbial for cunning craftiness, and thus J is provided with a convenient symbol for his parable (cf. Matt. 10.16). SUBTIL: wily, insidious, crafty. In reading this parable we should not identify the serpent with Satan or a personal Devil, for such a conception did not arise until after the Exile; the earliest identification occurs in Wisdom 2.24; so also Rev. 12.9; 20.2. The SERPENT of J's parable is a personification *symbol of evil* of temptation, and is not to be thought of as something external to our nature. We should notice that J is not attempting to answer a philosophical question: Where does evil come from? How did evil gain an entry into God's good world? He is vividly portraying our actual human condition; he is describing things as they are, not offering theories to explain them. His parable is not a kind of philosophical allegory.

4. Ye shall not surely die

The serpent cunningly appeals to human vanity and artfully suggests a doubt about the goodness of God. Man's

proneness to exalt himself as over against God can be
bolstered up by disbelief in God's love. Rebellion can be
justified by intellectual arguments; pride goes hand in hand
with scepticism. To disobey and to doubt are parallel processes. The Bible everywhere maintains that faith is a virtue
and unbelief is a sin; this is a difficult doctrine for modern
people brought up in the (false) notion that everyone has a
right to believe what he likes. Kierkegaard was right: 'It
is so hard to believe because it is so hard to obey.' We
desire to assert ourselves, to emancipate ourselves from
obedience to God's law. God makes demands upon us: he
bids us worship him, not ourselves; he commands us to love
others as ourselves; his aweful holiness judges us and
'shows us up'. Therefore we listen the more eagerly to
the sceptics who give us excellent reasons why we should
doubt his goodness or even his existence: self-assertion
is the parent of unbelief. How clearly J perceives that our
'reasons' are rationalizations, that pride is the father of
doubt. The serpent suggests to the woman that God did
not forbid the eating of the tree of knowledge out of any
concern for human well-being, but because he wished to
preserve his divinity for himself; he did not wish to share
it with his creatures. Therefore he pretended that there
was a dreadful penalty attached to the eating of the fruit,
namely, death. But actually the contrary is the truth: to
eat of the tree of knowledge confers the power to be AS GOD.
This is the fatal weakness of human nature: man's desire
to give the glory to himself and not to the Creator, to usurp
the place of God and put himself at the centre of the
universe, to set himself up in the position which belongs to
God alone. The Bible and the whole Christian tradition
teach that the basic sin is pride. Pride is the root and
essence of all human sinfulness and rebellion against
God. The J writer strikingly brings out this truth in his
parable.

PRIDE
SIN

5. ye shall be as God

For the use of the plural form of the name of GOD see on
1.1 and 1.26. Man snatches at equality with God: such is
his pride; contrast Phil. 2.6—Christ, 'the Last Adam',
counted it not a prize to be on an equality with God, but
took the form of a servant: such is his humility.

knowing good and evil

That is, knowing all things, but in the Hebrew sense of
KNOWING—not 'academic' knowledge but practical experience that comes by doing everything, good and bad (see note
on 2.9, THE TREE OF THE KNOWLEDGE OF GOOD AND EVIL).
It is implied that man aims at being AS GOD in the sense
of making his own good and evil, determining for himself
what is good and evil, unwilling to allow God to determine
what is right and wrong.

7. the eyes of them both were opened

But not in the way that the serpent had promised in v. 5!
The serpent had suggested that man could help himself to
the knowledge of things as they are. The Bible knows that
men cannot do this; God alone is the source of all true knowledge. The N.T. strongly emphasizes this truth by its representation of Christ as the Opener of the Blind Eyes. In the
parable, the opening of the eyes of the man and the woman
means their realization of their sinfulness: they are ashamed
in the presence of each other (we always try to hide our
wrong-doing from our fellows under futile pretensions—
mere fig-leaves!—of virtue).

8. the LORD God walking in the garden

On this delightful and bold anthropomorphism see the
Introduction above. J does not, of course, think of God as
a physical being who can 'walk' and 'talk': the story is
a *parable* and it was not intended that it should be taken
literally.

the man and his wife hid themselves

Not only are guilty men ashamed in the presence of their
✳fellows, but they are ashamed in the presence of God.   They
try to hide themselves from him—in all sorts of ways.   They
can hide themselves so successfully (as it seems) that they can
even come to imagine that he does not exist!   And yet, just
when they feel safest, they are liable to hear the disturbing,
accusing voice of the Holy God.

12, 13. Man is adept at shifting responsibility from himself.
In the parable the man blames the woman, the woman
blames the serpent.   But nothing can remove human responsibility, since to be human (as we have seen) is to be responsible.   Man's being is defined, according to the Bible, by the
fact that he *answers* (one way or another) the address of God.

14. It is probably a mistake to suppose that J holds that the
characteristics of serpents are derived from the guilt of their
ancestor in the Garden of Eden.   His story is much more
profound than that.   He perceives that there is mystery in
the wretchedness and bestiality of so much of the brute
creation (here represented by the serpent).   'The whole
creation groaneth and travaileth in pain together until now'
(Rom. 8.22).   He knows that somehow this mystery is connected with the entry of sin into the world, the cosmic rebellion against God's good purpose.   But he is wise enough
to state the mystery in the form of a parable and to refrain
from attempting an explanation of it.

15. enmity between thee and the woman. . . .

Whereas according to the divine intention the whole
animal creation should have lived harmoniously under the
beneficent dominion of man, an attitude of mutual hostility
has developed and men and beasts prey upon one another.
'Nature red in tooth and claw' is the result not of the
Creator's design but of the entry of sin into the world.

it shall bruise thy head

The old Christian commentators called this clause *Protevangelium*, that is, the first proclamation of the gospel of redemption. God promises that the seed of the woman shall crush the serpent's head, i.e., obtain victory over temptation and evil. They regarded this promise as the first recorded prophecy of the redemption to be wrought by Christ: the Son of Mary would deliver from the power of sin the fallen sons of Eve. The J writer, of course, had no such clear-cut prophecy in mind, but perhaps he is here hinting in his parable at the ultimate redemption of the human race, and Christians will rightly interpret his unformulated hope as having found its realization in Christ's victory over sin and death.

thou shalt bruise his heel

A suggestive metaphor: man, afflicted by his sin, limps along the road of life, unable to speed his progress towards his true goal.

16. in sorrow thou shalt bring forth children

The travail of child-birth is no part of the Creator's beneficent intention, but is a result of the disorder which sin has brought about. This strange world of ours is compounded of pain and pleasure, sorrow and joy: woman accepts the 'sorrows of Eve'—her desire is for her husband—and 'when she is delivered of the child, she remembereth no more the anguish, for the joy that a man is born into the world' (John 16.21). The woman's child-bearing is a sharing of the redemptive burden that must be borne (I Tim. 2.15). Mary's *Magnificat* (Luke 1.46-55) is her expression of gratitude for her unique privilege in the bearing of the burden of redemption and of her joy that THE MAN is born into the world; the whole Church has rejoiced with her to sing *Magnificat*; all generations of Christians have called her Blessed.

he shall rule over thee

The irksomeness of the authority of the man is the consequence of sin; see note on 2.23.

17. cursed is the ground

The sentence passed upon the woman is now followed by one upon the man. His days shall be filled with toil, and toil will be irksome. As we have seen (see notes on 2.8 and 2.15), work itself is not a curse; but it becomes a curse to man by reason of his sin. That which should have been a glad co-operation with God—the dressing and keeping of the garden—becomes a laborious and uncongenial task amongst the thorns and thistles of the field. How true this biblical insight remains in the world of work as we know it to-day! The working life of man, the whole sphere of industry and commerce, instead of being the happy fellowship of mutual aid amongst brothers, as it ought to be, is embittered by men's sordid profit-seeking, lust for domination, fratricidal quarrelling and group selfishness. Our world of large-scale industry and mechanized farming is changed beyond all recognition from the world that J knew; yet man's heart has not changed, and J's insight is as valid to-day as it was 3,000 years ago. The Bible teaches that work is a divine ordinance for mankind, and that in its faithful performance man fulfils the intention of the Creator for human life. When work is done ' as unto the Lord ', it is a source of deep satisfaction and joy (cf. Eph. 6.5-9, etc.; on this whole subject see Alan Richardson, *The Biblical Doctrine of Work*, London, 1952).

19. dust thou art, and unto dust shalt thou return

God's sentence on man now reaches its climax: it is the sentence of death. The Bible consistently teaches that death is the result of sin: ' in Adam all die ' (I Cor. 15.22; cf. Rom. 5.12); ' the wages of sin is death ' (Rom. 6.23). The Bible knows nothing of an immortal soul in man (see notes on 2.7),

and the death sentence is passed on the whole man, all there
is of him (despite Longfellow!). The Bible everywhere
takes death seriously; it is a real passing into non-being,
not simply a change of state. Nothing but a miracle can
bring man into being again—an act of new creation. This
act of new creation has happened in Christ: if any man be
in Christ he is—quite literally—a new creation (II Cor.
5.17): Christian baptism is a real death and a real new
birth to the life of the age to come (Rom. 6.3-10).

20. Eve

The Hebrew word (*Havvah*) means 'Living', 'Life' (RV
margin). Man, sentenced to death, about to be expelled
from paradise, with heroic hope names his wife 'Life'—
the life that goes on, in spite of death. 'Where there
is life there is hope', and man is not bereft of hope in
spite of all the failures and disappointments of his mortal
lot.

21. coats of skins

This is no mere childish speculation about the origin of
clothing, as the old-fashioned commentaries tell us. Man
stands guilty and ashamed before God, yet God respects him
in his shame and clothes him with his own hand. Thus
man may stand again in the awareness of God—not in the
old relationship of innocence but in the relationship of
'religion' (so W. Vischer, p. 65; 'what is religion but man's
sense of shame before God, and his attempt to clothe himself in his presence? '); nor yet in the new relationship that
Christ establishes—clothed with righteousness (cf. II Cor.
5.2). It is of God's merciful goodness that man the sinner
is still present to him, his nakedness covered. But there is
a further insight here. God drives man out of paradise, but
he does not abandon him. He preserves his life; all the
'orders of preservation', by which human life—even the
lives of pagans, blasphemers, atheists, and so on—is kept in

existence, are in truth evidences of the gracious providence
of God which surrounds our sinful race.

22. the man is become as one of us

For the plural form of the divine being see notes on 1.1
and 1.26. Cf. also 3.5. The phrase means that man has
become a responsible being—like the angelic beings who
inhabit the heavenly court. But being sinful he must not
for ever possess attributes and powers which he would ter-
ribly abuse. Such a being must not continue for ever; his
existence must be brought to an end. But God has made
provision for his ultimate redemption and re-creation. Man
is to TILL THE GROUND FROM WHENCE HE WAS TAKEN until
such time as he may be brought to himself and re-made in
the image of God. For the TREE OF LIFE see note on 2.9.

24. the Cherubim, and the flame of a sword

Cherub (plural, *cherubim*) is a winged sphinx with a
human head, appearing frequently in Mesopotamian mythology from early times. In the O.T. it is a symbol denoting
God's presence in majesty (e.g. Ps. 18.10). The CHERUBIM
here are appropriate to the poetical form of the parable, as
also is THE FLAME OF A SWORD (lit. ' the flame of a whirling
sword '). God's decree of expulsion from paradise is en-
forced by his active power and majesty. Man's attempts
to build a Utopia on the earth, free from drudgery and pain,
are doomed to failure. The reason is no arbitrary divine
decree, but the fact that man is unfit to live in paradise. He
has made God's good world a place of strife and rivalry—
as the story of Cain and Abel immediately goes on to show
—and the road of redemption is long and steep. But nevertheless man must struggle forward, and there is promise of
reward in the struggle. Every effort to wipe the sweat from
the face of man, to uproot the thorns and thistles in the field
of his labour, to relieve pain and increase joy, will not be in
vain; the seed of woman will bruise the serpent's head. In

Christ the full assurance of this promise is given by God to all the toiling sons of Eve.

So the parable ends. With astonishing insight it has laid bare the nature of man's predicament as a being capable of response to the divine address, yet incapable of fulfilling in his own strength the divine command and intention. It has presented us with a prologue to the whole biblical drama of our salvation. The leading *motifs* of that drama are adumbrated in it; the fundamental situation of man as over against God is depicted with amazing clarity and skill. Man stands a rebel against his Creator, refusing to give God the glory; yet God will not let man go, or allow him to suffer the full and dire consequences of his rebellion. Though he punishes, God is ever preserving man's life from destruction and preparing the way of salvation; his chastening is but the 'rod and staff' in the hand of the faithful Shepherd who seeks to lead us to himself.

III

CAIN AND ABEL
4.1-16; J

It is difficult to determine precisely what literary relation
this legend bears to the preceding parable of Creation and
Fall. Both come from the J source. In many ways this
story seems to present in another form the truth of the Fall
of Man. It does not follow quite naturally upon the preceding story, since several of its details do not entirely harmonize with the details of the parable of the Fall. Adam was
sentenced to till the ground, but one of his sons (Abel) does
not do this. Again we seem to be reading of an expulsion
from Eden (vv. 14, 16). And it is implied that the earth is
already inhabited by people who are presumably not Cain's
brethren. Perhaps the explanation is that J's stories were
originally told separately from one another, each complete
in itself and carrying its own lesson, no attempt being made
to harmonize them with one another in detail. Such an
attempt would not be necessary until at last they came to be
written down and arranged (as we have them) in a consecutive order. The editor (whoever he was) may have done
considerable work in this direction, but we may be grateful
to him that he did not carry the process to the point of
destroying the individuality of his stories. As now arranged
the story shows how fratricidal strife is the consequence of
man's rebellion against God, that Adam's sin opens the way
for the sin of his first-born son.

1. the man knew Eve his wife

In the O.T. the word 'know' (*yadha'*) is used of sexual

intercourse. This is not mere euphemism. In Hebrew thought 'knowing' is not merely academic or 'intellectual'; it always involves entering into active personal relations with the person known. In this sense sexual knowledge is the fullest, truest and most satisfying kind of knowledge that exists—and all this must be understood to be implied in passages where the knowledge of God is spoken of. It is significant that the most intimate knowledge of God that Israel has is often represented under the form of the Lover-Loved or Husband-Wife relationship. Cf. such passages as: 'You only have I *known* . . .' (Amos 3.2). Sex knowledge is for the Bible the exemplar of true knowledge (*v.* Otto Piper, *The Christian Interpretation of Sex*, London, 1942, pp. 52ff.). This is the basic truth which Freud has distorted in representing all knowledge as sexual.

Cain

It is doubtful what the word means, but it has assonance with *ganah*, to get. Eve expresses her joy at the birth of her first-born; cf. John 16.21. She acknowledges the truth which the Bible constantly teaches, that children are 'a heritage and gift that cometh of the LORD' (Ps. 127.3; cf. Ps. 128).

Abel

The name (whatever might be its origin) would suggest *Hebel*, a breath—something that quickly passes away; it would emphasize the brevity and feebleness of human life; cf. Ps. 39.5: 'Surely every man at his best is altogether a breath' (RV margin).

3. an offering

Hebrew *minhah*—a gift offered to a superior as an expression of gratitude for his good-will (later specifically the 'meal offering', e.g., Lev. 2.1). J takes sacrifice for granted as not needing any explanation, long before its institution by Moses! It is a natural thing for men to do. Both Cain

and Abel bring the product of their labours as an oblation
to Jehovah.

4, 5. We are not told why Abel's offering was acceptable and
Cain's was not. Perhaps J wished to teach that the correct
form of sacrifice was that of animals; but long after his time
' vegetarian ' offerings were also made. Most commentators
assume that it was the *attitude* of Cain which was wrong;
perhaps Cain was proudly confident that his offering was
better than his brother's. He was justifying himself before
God by his ' works ', and he did not reflect that the offerings
we bring to God are God's own gifts to us and we must not
take pride in them. Abel approached God in humility,
trusting solely in God's gracious goodness to make man's
unworthy offering acceptable to himself. So Heb. 11.4
seems to interpret the matter: ' by *faith* Abel offered unto
God a more excellent sacrifice than Cain, through which
he had witness borne to him that he was righteous, God
bearing witness in respect of his gifts: and through it he
being dead yet speaketh'. Though the Greek text of
Hebrews in this verse is not altogether certain, it would
seem to be implied that it was Abel's attitude of faith in
God's righteousness, and not (like Cain's) in his own, that
made his oblation acceptable; thus Abel still teaches us the
right spirit in which to approach God when we come before
him with our gifts. If this is the correct interpretation of
J's words, it is clear that he has anticipated much of the
later prophetic teaching about sacrifice.

5. Cain was very wroth
    That something was very wrong with Cain's attitude
is clearly implied by J, which supports our interpretation of
the divine rejection of his offering.

7. unto thee shall be his desire
    The RV does not make good sense of this passage, which

means: Sin crouches like a wild beast at the door, ready to spring upon you, for it desires to possess you; but you must control it.

9. my brother's keeper
The very first question that man addresses to God in the Bible is a petulant questioning of his responsibility for his brother. The Bible teaches that to be human is to be responsible (see note on 1.26), responsible to God. J shows here that to be responsible to God means to be responsible for one's brother. The Bible does not talk about respecting human personality because it is 'sacred'; we are to love and respect others not because they possess sacred rights or are valuable in themselves, but because God loves them (cf. I Cor. 8.11, 'the brother for whose sake Christ died'). See also note on 9.6.

10. thy brother's blood crieth unto me
In ancient Israel it was the duty of the next-of-kin of a murdered man to avenge his death, to be his vindicator (*go'el*). God reveals himself as Abel's *go'el*, as the 'next-of-kin' to every victim of injustice. There is wonderful insight here. But the Bible goes on to tell of another Victim whose blood spilt cries not for vengeance but for pardon (Heb. 12.24):

> Abel's blood for vengeance
> Pleaded to the skies;
> But the Blood of Jesus
> For our pardon cries.

11. the ground
Probably the good, cultivated land: Cain is cursed and driven away from it. THE GROUND here may be Eden, from which Cain is being expelled; he goes off to the east of Eden (v. 16). Or perhaps THE GROUND is thought of as the Holy Land.

12. Cf. Gen. 3.17, ' Cursed is the ground for thy sake.' J discerns that ' the Fall ' is of cosmic significance; the mystery of evil pervades all nature as well as all human life.

13. My punishment is greater than I can bear

Or (with RV margin), ' My iniquity is greater than can be forgiven '—a possible translation. But the words of the RV text are more in keeping with the character of Cain. The next verse suggests that Cain is full of self-pity rather than of remorse: WHOSOEVER FINDETH ME SHALL SLAY ME.

14. from thy face shall I be hid

Perhaps God is held to be specially present in the (Holy) ground, and Cain as a wanderer in distant lands would be separated from him. But certainly the words symbolize the truth that sin shuts man out from the presence of the Holy God.

15. a sign for Cain

The Bible is the book of covenant, and this verse records the first covenant which God makes with man (though the actual word ' covenant ' is not used in this passage). It is significant that the covenant is made with *sinful* man—with the man who is his brother's murderer. Here lies the supreme miracle and mystery of grace. God will not let man go or abandon him to his justly merited fate: Cain in his wanderings—even far away from the presence of God— nevertheless stands under the protection of God. In his merciful goodness God sets up the ' orders of preservation ' which enable the life of sinful humanity to continue (see also notes on 3.21 and 9.6, 11). And this is the miracle of grace: that God becomes *go'el* not only for the innocent victim but even for the murderer, that is, for fallen man as such. For just as Adam is everyman, so also is Cain; we are all responsible for our brother's death at every moment of our lives; everyman is his brother's murderer (cf. Matt. 5.21f.).

God undertakes voluntarily to be Cain's *go'el*, and appoints
a sign of the covenant with which he thus binds himself
(cf. the sign of the rainbow in the covenant with Noah,
Gen. 9.12-17; the sign of circumcision in the covenant with
Abraham, Gen. 17.11; etc.). We are not told in the case of
Cain what form the sign or token took. Perhaps it was a
sign such as that with which slaves were branded in the
ancient world, denoting that Cain was the slave of God (the
name *Cain* resembles the Arabic *gain-el*, 'slave of God').
The whole human race, even when it wanders far from the
face of God, still bears the mark of his ownership and the
token of his protection and loving-kindness. W. Vischer
(pp 74f) has (perhaps over-ingeniously) conjectured that
the mark of Cain, the ancient Israelite sign of Jehovah's
possession, was the mark *taw* (i.e., a cross) which in Ezekiel's
vision was set on the foreheads of faithful Jews who had
resisted the heathen abominations (Ezek. 9.4). In Christian
baptism the sign of the cross (cf. Rev. 7.3; 9.4) was invested
with a new and deeper significance as the sign of the New
Covenant of God with man, and those who were 'sealed'
with this sign became the 'slaves' of the Lord Jesus Christ
(Phil. 1.1, 'slaves of Christ Jesus', etc.; Gal. 6.17).

16. Nod
   i.e., 'wandering'—probably not a known place-name,
but an allegorical name signifying 'wandering from God's
presence'. No 'land of Nod' is known to historical
geography.

IV

CANAANITE CIVILIZATION
4.17-24; J

The biblical attitude towards civilization is ambiguous. All the gifts and blessings of civilization are from God; yet the advance of civilization does not of itself make men more reverent towards God or more humane towards one another. Every new invention or art of civilization—from the discovery of copper and iron (4.22) to that of nuclear fission—can be and has been turned to man's destruction and hurt. The growth of civilization is recounted in this section, but we must not look for any precise archæological information here, any more than we look to Gen. 1 for precise geological information. The narrator is telling the story of human development in the form of *saga*, not science. Cain's sons are prohibited from agriculture by the divine curse. Thus the pastorally and agriculturally minded Hebrews regard the civilization around them, with its cities, its arts and crafts, as something rather abnormal; it is the handiwork of Cain, who founded city life (v. 17). It is under the mark of Cain —exiled from the face of God, excluded from the true cultus (Jehovah-worship), yet preserved from annihilation by the grace of God. This truly represents the whole biblical attitude towards what we would call 'secular' civilization. (See also on 11.1-9.)

17. Cain knew his wife

The old question 'Where did Cain's wife come from?' used to be part of the stock-in-trade of the rationalists. The problem no longer troubles us, for we have seen that Genesis gives us not precise factual history, but a meditation upon history as seen from the point of view of the Creator's intention for man.

Enoch
Not the Enoch of Seth's line (5.18-24), who WALKED WITH GOD.

20, 21. father, i.e., metaphorically; ' the precursor '.

22. Tubal-cain
Here CAIN perhaps means ' smith ', ' craftsman '

23, 24. LAMECH'S boastful and vindictive song underlines the perception of J that the advance of civilization does not make men more humane.

V

THE TRUE LINE
OF ADAM (SETH)
4.25f.; J

This is J's account of the establishment of the true line of
descent from Adam (P's account is contained in chap. 5).
Here the fundamental idea of *Church* appears for the first
time in the Bible. It is 'set' or 'appointed' (cf. note on
SETH below) in the midst of the world that is not-church.
It is the 'People of God' set amongst the nations (Gentiles,
heathen) of the world. The true Church goes back to Adam,
and the story of the whole Bible is the story of the Church.
The Church is always distinguished from the world (here
represented by Cainite civilization) and stands over against
it, in the world but not of it. The Book of Genesis tells of
the beginning of the age-long process of the separating of
Church from non-Church: Seth—Cain; Abraham—Lot;
Jacob—Esau; Israel—the nations. The rest of the Bible con-
tinues the story, and shows that within Israel itself separa-
tion must take place: the Remnant becomes the Church
within the Church. Finally and supremely the New Testament shows us the separating of the New Israel from the
Old in the Church of Jesus Christ.

25. Seth
There is the kind of play on words which the Hebrews
enjoyed between this name (*Sheth*) and the word *shath*
('appointed', 'set'). SETH is as it were appointed the firm
foundation of the Adamic Church.

26. Enosh

The name is a poetical word meaning ' man ' (e.g. Ps. 8.4 :
' What is *'enosh* that thou art mindful of him? ').

then began men to call upon the name of the LORD

This means: In the days of Enosh men began to invoke
God by his name Jahweh. J's view on this theme contrasts
strongly with that of E and P (see Introduction). The
Church in the Adamic age in J's view worshipped the one
true God under his proper name, and man (*'enosh*) lived in
full personal relationship with God.

VI

GENEALOGY
FROM ADAM TO NOAH
5.1-32; P

The editor of Genesis now inserts P's genealogy of the supposed ten generations between Adam and Noah. The stylized expressions with which we became familiar in Chapter I meet us again; indeed, 5.1f. is a recapitulation of the P Creation story. The ages of the patriarchs mentioned here are, of course, entirely fanciful; like most primitive peoples the Hebrews believed that there once was a time when men lived to a fabulous age. One of the objects of the genealogy is to suggest the passage of a considerable period of time—in our RV (following the Hebrew text) 1,656 years—between the Creation and the Flood. The period is 1,307 years in the Samaritan text and 2,242 in the LXX, as the ages of the patriarchs are not in all cases the same in these versions (see Introduction). The genealogy represents P's version of the true 'Church-line' from Adam to Noah.

2. called their name Adam

Note that the man and his wife are *together* called ADAM, i.e., Man—'the man from the ground' (*'adamah*). In the next verse ADAM seems to be used as the proper name of the man alone.

3. a son in his own likeness, after his image

This verse is very important because it shows conclusively that the 'image of God' in which Adam (man) was made

(1.26f., 5.1) was not obliterated by the Fall (sin). Adam transmits the *imago Dei* to SETH and to his posterity. See note on 1.26; cf. also 9.6.

6. Seth, Enosh

Cf. 4.25f.(J). P tells us nothing about the persons who appear in his genealogy save their names, ages and offspring. The only exception is in the case of ENOCH (vv. 22 and 24); v. 29 is no exception, since it is inserted by the editor from J.

9. Kenan

P does not mention Cain and Abel, unless KENAN (etymologically a derivative from *Cain*) is the same person as Cain. If Cain were in one tradition a great-grandson of Adam (as KENAN is here), this would solve such problems as whom Cain married. But KENAN here stands in the true Church-line from Adam to Noah, and this would destroy the whole symbolic significance of the figure of Cain as we find it in J.

21. Methuselah

In the Hebrew and LXX texts METHUSELAH is the longest-lived of all the patriarchs (969 years); hence his name has passed into our language as a symbol of fabulous longevity. According to the Samaritan text he lived for a mere 720 years!

22, 24. Enoch walked with God. . . .

This can hardly be the Enoch who was the son of Cain (4.17), unless there was much confusion between the J and P traditions (cf. Cain, Kenan). This ENOCH is 'the seventh from Adam', and stands in the true succession from Seth. To 'walk with God' is an O.T. expression for perfect fellowship with God and implies a holy and righteous life (cf. Gen 6.9; Micah 6.8; Mal. 2.6).

he was not; for God took him

HE WAS NOT means 'he suddenly disappeared and was

nowhere to be found'; cf. a similar reference to the sudden
disappearance of Nero ('the Beast') in Rev. 17.8, 11 ('is
not'). GOD TOOK HIM means that Enoch was miraculously
taken up ('assumed', 'translated') into heaven without
dying (cf. Elijah, II Kings 2.11). P does not tell us what was
the nature of Enoch's remarkable righteousness which thus
secured for him immortal life, and we must suppose that
there were legends in the tradition concerning his piety.
There are not dissimilar legends of assumption into heaven
in Babylonian mythology. In later apocalyptic literature
Enoch becomes the custodian of the secrets of heaven and
earth, a preacher of repentance and a prophet of future
events. In the N.T. traces of these later developments are
found in Heb. 11.5f. and Jude 14f.; cf. also Ecclus. 44.16;
49.14. The passage in Jude is a quotation from the apocalyptic Book of Enoch (c. 105-64 B.C.). Perhaps we can best
understand the strange figure of Enoch in P's genealogy as
a sign given by God amidst all the wickedness of the days
before the Flood that God is the rewarder of righteousness
and of steadfast faith in him (so Heb. 11.5f.).

28. Lamech
P's LAMECH is an altogether different character from the
LAMECH of J's Song (4.23f.).

29. Noah
This verse, which unexpectedly introduces ideas from the
J tradition (THE TOIL OF OUR HANDS; cf. 3.17, 19; THE
GROUND WHICH THE LORD HATH CURSED; cf. 3.17; 4.11) must
be an insertion by the editor from J; note the occurrence of
the divine name Jahweh. The word NOAH means 'rest',
but its assonance with *nahem,* 'to comfort', suggests to J's
mind the notion of the mitigation of the curse láid upon
Adam's seed because of Noah's righteousness (cf. 6.9).

32. For Noah and his sons see commentary on 9.18ff. below.

VII

THE FALLEN ANGELS

6.1-4; J

This strange fragment must have formed part of a larger whole, not preserved for us; it bears little relation to what immediately precedes and follows it. Why did the editor place it here; indeed, why did he retain it at all? At first sight it seems to be a fragment of pagan mythology, utterly at variance with the biblical view of God. Many ancient peoples held similar primitive notions about sexual intercourse between the gods and human beings; classical mythology abounds in such legends. The giants or supermen who were supposed to have existed in a remote heroic age (cf. the Greek Titans) were held to be the offspring of such divine-human intercourse. But why was such a story incorporated into the Bible? Would it not be better to expunge it altogether?

The answer is that the passage, though cast in a mythological form, contains an essentially biblical insight. Whatever its origin in prehistoric legend, it stands in the Bible because it expresses biblical truth. But it is not to be taken as literally true; it is a story with a deep symbolic significance. The men of the Bible took the facts of sin and evil seriously; 'the Fall' was not merely a human catastrophe but was cosmic in its scope, affecting the whole creation (Rom. 8.20-22). Like the story of Cain, this is in fact another version of the Fall story, bringing out still a further aspect of the matter. Evil is no mere defect of human nature which can be remedied by better education, better

93

sociological and political arrangements or better psychological techniques. It exists outside and beyond human
nature. There is a quality of the world and of life which
can be described only as *demonic*: that which is good and
admirable becomes inextricably intermingled with that
which is evil and horrifying. There is, as it were, a marriage
of the good and the bad, which produces the demonic—the
blended idealism and inhumanity of (say) Imperial Rome or
Soviet Russia, the 'greatness' of giant personalities (like
Alexander the Great or Napoleon or Lenin), who impose
their demonic will upon millions, or the commingled bene-
ficence and Satanic cruelty of 'systems', like capitalism or
bureaucracy or state-control. Nothing is ever purely good
or purely evil; the science which gives us penicillin gives us
also hydrogen bombs—and so on. This is what is meant by
the conception of the demonic, and it is this demonic quality
of the world that this story presents to us in mythological
form: it is because of this demonic feature of the world that
man's years on earth are numbered. The ancient narrator
of the legend, of course, did not think in our conceptual
terms; he thought in a mythological way and saw truth embodied in stories of angels and giants. He was untroubled
by our fuller knowledge: we know that there never was a
time when there were giants in the earth, and we must state
the inner meaning of the truth which he saw in our more
conceptualized way. But we must not explain away his
understanding of the sinister reality of cosmic evil or allow
ourselves to be persuaded that he was only a 'primitive
story-teller' whose message we have outgrown.

2. the sons of God

The phrase denotes the semi-divine, angelic beings who
frequent the court of heaven (cf. Job 1.6). They are not
stated to be evil or 'fallen', though it seems to be implied
in v. 3 that their association with the daughters of men
constitutes their 'fall'. This is certainly understood by the

writers of II Pet. 2.4 and Jude 6, who speak of the dire
punishment meted out to the angels who left their proper
habitations.

3. This verse is textually uncertain (see RV margin) and is
very difficult to interpret. Perhaps it means that man is
weak and feeble (FLESH) and God would not for ever continue to strive for his betterment or allow his SPIRIT (the
breath of life, Gen. 2.7) to remain in him; nevertheless in
his mercy God does not destroy man at once but allows
him to live out his span of 120 years. (Since the time of the
Flood man's span of life is 'three score years and ten', Ps.
90.10.)

4. The Nephilim

The derivation and meaning of the word are uncertain.
But the NEPHILIM are mentioned again in Num. 13.33, where
we learn that men are to them as grasshoppers are to men.
Further, the LXX translates the word *gigantes,* whence AV
'giants'. But the Greek word would carry a reference
beyond that of our English 'giants', who are merely very
big men. The Gigantes of Greek mythology were a race of
*super*human monsters who fought against the gods and were
defeated by them. The LXX uses *gigantes* again to trans-
late MIGHTY MEN. Though the NEPHILIM were superhuman
beings, the J writer nevertheless seems to identify them
with the legendary heroes (THE MEN OF RENOWN) whom
the Hebrews (like other races) believed to have existed in
primæval times (cf. Deut. 1.28; 2.10f., 21; 9.2; Amos 2.9).
They are symbols of the 'demonic' quality of 'great' men
in every age. See also note on 10.9.

VIII

THE FLOOD
6.5—9.17; J and P

In this section the story of Noah and the Flood sets before us the biblical view of a corrupt human race in which the number of the righteous (i.e. those relying upon God for their justification or salvation—not the self-righteous) is small. The Church is the faithful remnant, whether in the days of Noah or in later times, set in the midst of a world that is perishing: this is the view of the Bible as a whole, and it is the view of the Lord Jesus himself (Matt. 7.13f.; Luke 13.23f., etc.). The Church is the ark of salvation in which God saves those whom he has chosen from the wickedness and destruction of ' the world '; Noah's ark is a ' type ' or sign of the Church of the faithful in all the ages (cf. I Pet. 3.20f.). The covenant which God makes with Noah becomes the type of the ' covenant of peace ' which God makes with those who trust and obey him in every age (Isa. 54.9f.), and Noah himself becomes a biblical type of the ' preacher of righteousness ' (II Pet. 2.5) and of the man of faith who was saved through his trust in the promise of the Lord (Heb. 11.7). Modern folk who often hold sentimentalized notions about the love of God, based upon their failure to appreciate the horror and extent of sin, are apt to take offence at the biblical picture of mankind as perishing in its wickedness and at the thought of the awefulness of the divine judgment. Yet it was to the story of the Flood that our Lord turned for an illustration of the sudden and terrible destruction that would overtake the world at the coming (*parousia*) of the Son of Man (Matt. 24.37-39).

The legend of the Flood entered Palestine from a Babylonian source. There are many parallels between the Babylonian original and the biblical versions (see S. R. Driver, esp. pp. 103ff., where the Babylonian story is set out at length). In Genesis two versions of the story, those of J and P, have been conflated by the editor (see notes below). The difference between the Babylonian and the biblical versions is chiefly that in the latter what was originally a piece of primitive mythology has been turned into a magnificent presentation of the whole biblical conception of the awefulness of God's judgment and the wonderful quality of his mercy. As in the other Genesis stories, the representation of biblical truth takes parabolic form; there is no need to pretend that we are dealing with a (literally) true story. A great flood there may have been, especially in the Mesopotamian regions where the story probably originated, and in this sense the legend may be based on a folk-memory of an actual deluge; but modern science does not confirm the view that since the appearance of man the earth has been flooded to a depth of five miles all over its surface. Geologists now have other ways of accounting for the presence of marine fossils at high mountain altitudes. The story, like the creation stories, conveys truth in the form of parable. The wonder is that the divine revelation can take the primitive and childish speculations and legends of the pagan world and can make of them the vehicle of ultimate truth—truth expressed in a form which the ' pre-scientific ' contemporaries of J and P could grasp, and which can speak in every age to all who are willing to lay aside their sophistication and become as little children. Only those who are ' wise in their own conceits ' will think that they have nothing to learn from the divinely inspired children's story of Noah's Ark.

J's Introduction to the Parable of the Flood 6.5-8

Jehovah finds that his good intention in the creation of the world is frustrated by man's sin, he resolves to 'blot out' (DESTROY, v. 7) both man and his servants, the animal creation.

5. every imagination . . . of his heart was only evil

This is the *locus classicus* for the later rabbinic doctrine of the 'evil impulse' or 'evil imagination' (*yetzer ha-ra'*) which leads men to the two sins of idolatry and unchastity, always connected in biblical thought (cf. Rom. 1.20-32). (See W. D. Davies, *Paul and Rabbinic Judaism*, 1948, pp. 2-31; N. P. Williams, *Ideas of the Fall and of Original Sin*, 1927, Lecture II.) Belief in God in the O.T. is not an affair of the intellect only; it is the evil will (heart) which leads the head astray, and unbelief is sin, just as in the N.T. faith is a virtue, divinely implanted. The man who denies God (intellectually or practically) is morally corrupt (i.e., in O.T. language, a 'fool', Ps. 14.1).

6. it repented the LORD . . . and . . . grieved him

The Bible is not afraid of anthropomorphic language, and God is not impassible (incapable of emotion, grief and pain) as in Greek thought. Cf. Hos. 11 (esp. vv. 8f.); Luke 15, etc. Thus the Bible does not hesitate to speak of God's HEART, i.e., in Hebrew psychology, the centre of the personality, the emotions (love, etc.) and will.

8. Grace here (as often in O.T.) means 'favour', 'acceptance'.

P's Introduction to the Parable of the Flood 6.9-12

We note the change of style and recognize again the

stereotyped phrases of P (e.g. THESE ARE THE GENERATIONS
OF . . . AFTER THEIR KIND) throughout the remainder of this
chapter. This section corresponds to the above section of
J and likewise emphasizes the corruption of the world and
the righteousness of Noah.

9. perfect, blameless (R.V. margin); cf. Job 1.1.

Noah walked with God, cf. 5.22, 24.

10. For Noah's sons see on 9.18.

NOAH BUILDS THE ARK (P)
6.13-22

13. The end of all flesh is come before me
This means: 'The end of mankind has come into my
mind and I have decided upon it' (cf. J's words in v. 7).
ALL FLESH, a stereotyped phrase in P (thirteen times in his
Flood story), means 'all mankind' here and in v. 12, etc.,
but sometimes it means the animal world (6.19; 7.15f.; 8.17)
and sometimes both men and animals (6.17; 7.21; 9.11).

14. an ark of gopher wood
An ARK (Heb. *tebah*, a word of Egyptian origin) is not
a ship, which has means of propulsion (sails, oars) and steer-
ing, but a large floating crate. The Hebrews had no seafaring experience, and hence they had only sketchy notions
of what would be required for the construction of a sea-
going vessel; it is interesting to note that in the Babylonian
story the vessel is a *ship*. GOPHER WOOD may be pine.

rooms, i.e., compartments (lit. 'nests', RV margin).

15. The dimensions of the ARK are approximately 450 ft.
by 75 ft. by 45 ft. This is nearly half the length of the
Queen Elizabeth and more than half the breadth (987 ft. by
118 ft.); the ARK, of course, was oblong in shape.

16. A light
Probably an opening running all round the vessel at the
top just below the roof, which would be supported by posts.

18. my covenant
This is the first appearance of this fundamental word of
the biblical revelation; for the explication of it see notes on
9.1-17, where the content of the COVENANT with Noah is dis-
cussed.

19. two of every sort
Contrast 7.2 and see note *ad loc.*

21. P pictures mankind as vegetarian before the Flood (see
note on 9.3). Cf. also 1.29f.

THE DELUGE (J and P)
7.1-24

For this section the editor has taken portions from J and
from P and has combined them into one story, but he has
not taken the trouble to harmonize all the details, as we
shall see. A few sentences have been composed by the
editor himself to provide connections or explanations between the different elements from J and P.

THE ENTRY INTO THE ARK (mostly J)
7.1-10

2. of every clean beast . . . seven and seven
P scrupulously avoids the mention of all Levitical institutions (such as the distinction between clean and unclean
beasts) before the giving of the Law to Moses at Sinai. J,
on the other hand, assumes that such institutions (cf. also
sacrifice) are older than the Flood, and doubtless J is right—
the distinction runs right back into prehistory. P's stream-

lined history endeavours to give Mosaic origin and sanction to what in fact had existed from immemorial antiquity. Thus P says that Noah was commanded to take only a pair of every species into the ark, while J says he was bidden to take seven pairs of clean and a pair of unclean creatures. In the N.T. the abolition of the distinction between clean and unclean meats by Jesus (Mark 7.14-19) and his Church (Acts 10.9-16; Rom. 14, etc.) is one of the most obvious, if not the most profound, of the breaches with the theory and practice of Judaism. The distinction was, of course, one of ritual, not of hygiene, and its origins are to be sought in the most primitive religious ideas of mankind; but throughout the long history of Judaism (until to-day) it was observed with meticulous care and valued as an outward badge or symbol of Jewish separateness from the Gentile world. No such distinction could be tolerated in the Christian Church, where Jew and Gentile were one in Christ Jesus. If J is right in point of history, P is right in the matter of theology: God did not *create* some animals clean and some unclean, for when he looked upon EVERY THING THAT HE HAD MADE, BE-HOLD, IT WAS VERY GOOD (Gen. 1.31). In the N.T. the divine intention in the creation is restored: 'what God hath cleansed, make not thou common' (Acts 10.15).

6. This verse is inserted into the J material from the P source by the editor; it clearly belongs to the genealogical compilation which has been used in Chapter 5.

THE WATERS PREVAIL (mostly P)
7.11-24

In this section the editor has conflated his two sources; from P he seems to have derived vv. 11, 13-16 (except in v. 16 the words AND THE LORD SHUT HIM IN), 18-21, and 24. The remainder is from J. The principal discrepancy between the two accounts, which the editor has not troubled

to cover up, concerns the duration of the Flood. In P the
waters prevail for 150 days, and remain on the earth for a
year and eleven days altogether; in J they increase forty
days and forty nights, and then disappear after three weeks,
thus remaining on the earth for sixty-one days altogether
(see S. R. Driver, pp. 85f. for details).

11. the fountains of the great deep
According to P some upheaval causes 'the waters that
are under the earth' to burst forth in great water-spouts; in
J only the rain is mentioned. See note on 1.9-13 above.

the windows of heaven
The openings in the great inverted basin of the sky out of
which it was believed that the rain came. See note on 1.6
above.

16. the LORD shut him in
A delightful anthropomorphism—obviously from J: note
the occurrence of the name *Jahweh.*

22. the breath of the spirit of life
A tautology, lit. 'the spirit of the spirit of life'; Hebrew
ruach, as in 2.7 (J), 6.17 and 7.15 (P). The expression is
unique and may be due to some early copyist's error.

THE WATERS DECREASE (P)
8.1-5

Only the first half of v. 3 is from J.

4. the mountains of Ararat
The mountains of the modern Armenia were the highest
known to the peoples of Palestine and Mesopotamia, and so
naturally would be chosen as the point at which the ark
would ground. The modern 'Mount Ararat' (16,969 ft.) on

the borders of Turkey, Iran and the U.S.S.R. is the traditional site of the episode. Its summit stands some 4,000 feet
above the permanent snow-line.

THE FACE OF THE GROUND IS DRIED (J)
8.6-14

Only the calendar details in v. 13 (first half) and v. 14 are
from P.

7. a raven

An example of an ' unclean' creature (Lev. 11.15; Deut.
14.14). The Hebrew implies that the bird went out and
stayed away, doubtless feeding on carcases. The bird is one
of evil omen amongst the Arabs, but not in the O.T.

8. a dove

A ' clean' creature, and one of which the Hebrew tradition
speaks affectionately. It is noted for its harmlessness (Matt.
10.16), for its plaintive cooing (Isa. 38.14; 59.11) and for its
foolishness (Hos. 7.11). In the N.T. it becomes part of the
symbolism of the baptismal theology of the early Church,
representing the Holy Spirit (Mark 1.10). Possibly the symbolism bears some reference to this verse, since the deliverance of Noah was thought of as a ' baptism' of the human
race (I Pet. 3.20f.), but there is no reason to suppose that the
dove here carries any symbolic reference to the Spirit of
God. It is just another of the delightful incidents in the
parable.

11. an olive leaf pluckt off

Or ' a fresh olive leaf' (RV margin), in either case a sign
of the revivification of the order of nature. It is curious
that in our language to ' bear an olive-branch' has become
a familiar expression meaning to offer or to sue for peace—
and the phrase is based on this text. But here we read of a

LEAF, not a branch; and the DOVE is not offering or suing
for peace. The OLIVE LEAF is, however, a sign that God's
wrath is past and in that sense it may be said to be an
emblem of peace.

THE GOING FORTH FROM THE ARK (P)
8.15-19

Note the repetition of the characteristic phrases of P.

GOD'S PROMISE TO NOAH (J)
8.20-22

This passage is J's version of a theme which is more fully
dealt with in P's account of God's Covenant with Noah
(9.1-17).

20. burnt offerings on the altar

As noted above, J thinks of sacrifice as in existence long
before the institution of the sacrifices of the Law under
Moses; cf. 4.3f.; 12.8. The *'olah* (whole burnt offering) was
a sacrifice in which the whole carcase 'went up', i.e., was
consumed by fire; the word *'olah* comes from *'alah*, which
means ' go up'. Only ' clean' creatures could, of course, be
used in sacrifice, and Noah had taken seven pairs of each
of these (according to J : cf. 7.2).

21. the LORD smelled the sweet savour

That is, Jahweh accepted the offering (cf. 4.4, THE LORD
HAD RESPECT UNTO ABEL AND TO HIS OFFERING); lit., ' Jahweh
smelled the savour of gratification' (cf. Lev. 1.9, 13, 17,
etc., where regulations concerning the burnt-offering are laid
down).

the LORD said in his heart

That is, ' Jahweh said to himself'; cf. 6.6.

I will not again curse the ground

The reference is, of course, to 3.17 (cf. 4.12); Noah is thought of as having by his righteousness (in faith) secured the amelioration of the lot of mankind.

the imagination of man's heart is evil

See note on 6.5.

neither will I smite again

God's promise to Noah is one of forbearance: man is evil FROM HIS YOUTH (i.e. from the moment when he is old enough to discern right and wrong), yet God in his merciful and long-suffering graciousness not only will not destroy mankind but (as the next verse implies) will make provision for the continuance and sustentation of man's life upon the earth. This theme is treated much more fully in the next section, which is taken from P.

GOD'S COVENANT WITH NOAH (P)
9.1-17

The idea of *covenant* is fundamental to the whole Bible, which indeed from the end of the second century A.D. has been thought of in the Christian Church as consisting of two covenants: the Hebrew *berith* (Gk. *diathēkē*) is often translated *testamentum* in the Vulgate; hence our 'Old Testament' and 'New Testament'. The meaning of these titles would be clearer if the word 'covenant' could be substituted for 'testament'.

Many covenants (some of them between men and men) are mentioned in the O.T. In the minds of the prophets the fundamental covenant is that of Horeb-Sinai (Exod. 19), ratified in the blood of the sacrificed animals (Exod. 24.8). In the N.T. a new covenant (Heb. 9.15) is made and ratified in the blood of Jesus Christ (Mark 14.24). It is regarded as right and proper that a covenant should be sealed or ratified in blood (i.e. with sacrifice: Ps. 50.5), though this is by no means a necessary feature of covenanting. P is precluded by his historical scheme from thinking of Noah's covenant as being ratified with sacrifice; but J in 8.20f. (though he does not use the word 'covenant') may have something of the kind in his mind in his account of Noah's altar of sacrifice.

The idea of COVENANT is fundamental in (and distinctive of) biblical religion because it implies a peculiar relationship between God and man. It implies a *binding* of two parties, a linking together of two dissimilar or hitherto unrelated persons or groups (there could be no covenants between brethren). Thus the distinction is retained between God and man, while at the same time their binding together is emphasized. The word *berith* (covenant) is probably the equivalent of the Assyrian *biritu*, 'bond' or 'fetter', though there is no unanimity about the etymology of the word. God *binds* himself to his people, but this is a voluntary act of God's grace: he had no obligations towards them and they had no claim upon him. The parties to the covenant are not equals; it is of the infinite grace and mercy of God that he binds himself in a covenant which he will not break.

Of the three principal covenants recorded in the Pentateuch the covenant with Noah, the covenant with Abraham (Gen. 17) and the covenant at Horeb-Sinai (Exod. 19), the two latter are covenants with *Israel* (though in each blessings are implied for all mankind). But the covenant with Noah is a covenant with all mankind, for now Noah virtually replaces Adam as the ancestor of the human race (indeed in Ecclus. 17.12 it is stated that in the creation God entered into a covenant with man as such). Through this covenant God provides for the preservation of mankind not only in the matter of food and warmth and bodily needs, nor yet only in respect of protection from disaster (such as the Flood itself) or natural enemies (the beasts); he also ordains and

sets up the order of society and government, without which
human life could not survive. This covenant, it is stressed,
is made with man as man, who is created in the image of
God (9.6)—it is not, that is to say, a covenant with a *church*,
a chosen group within the wider whole (Israel—old or new):
it is a covenant with mankind as a whole. Without the
constant covenanted care and protection of God, whether
men recognize the fact or not, human life could not continue
for a single day. But God requires that man on his part
shall fulfil the law that is ordained for him. This is not the
revealed Law of Moses, but that elementary knowledge of
right and wrong, the law of conscience, which even the
Gentiles possess (Rom. 2.14f.; Amos 2.1, etc.). All men
have conscience in the sense that they are aware of the
distinction between right and wrong and are aware also of
pressure to do the right. This knowledge is divinely implanted and is the beginning of man's knowledge of God.
No man is cut off from the knowledge of God, save by his
own depravity: no man is beyond the care and loving-
kindness of God, despite his depravity: all this is implied
in the covenant which God established between himself and
ALL FLESH that is on the earth.

1. Be fruitful and multiply

Cf. 1.28: God's purpose for mankind is not altered but is
re-established.

2. the fear and the dread of you . . .

Man's lordship over the animals is restored to him; indeed, it is made more emphatic than in 1.28. Primitive men
lived in constant dread of wild beasts; now man's *dominium*
is to be demonstrated by the fear and dread which the beasts
have for him. It is perhaps implied that the old, natural
relationship of man and the beasts, envisaged in Chapter I,
can now no longer continue: in God's original creation
everything obeyed the law of its being and so took its proper
place without conflict or disharmony in the grand hierarchy

of all created things; but now, after sin has disturbed the harmony of the creation, a new attitude of fear and dread has supervened. The prophets and apocalyptists look forward to the day when the disharmonies of the natural order shall be done away, when the leopard shall lie down with the kid and the lion eat straw like the ox; when, in fact, God's original intention in the creation shall be restored (Isa. 11.6-9).

4. the life . . . the blood

Life is sacred, and even when animals are killed and eaten care must be taken not to eat the blood, because it was held that *life* resides in the blood: 'the blood is the life' (Lev. 17.11, 14; Deut. 12.23). Hence it became a fundamental principle of Levitical legislation that all the blood must be drained off before the meat is eaten (Lev. 7.27; 17.10, 14), and the practice of eating only specially prepared meat ('kosher meat', from Heb. *kathar*, 'to be right', i.e. pure) is still continued by strict Jews to-day. The principle is regarded not as 'merely' ceremonial, but as moral, here and elsewhere in the O.T. (cf. Ezek. 33.25). [A similar belief has led other primitive peoples to drink the blood, as it were mystically, in order to identify themselves with and to acquire the life of the (totem) animal.] P is evidently aware that the practice is much older than Moses, and he traces its origin to God's covenant with Noah; in his view, therefore, it is binding on all mankind. Such ideas may seem to us to be crude and even superstitious, but unless we try sympathetically to understand them, we shall never appreciate the richness of the biblical symbolism of blood—blood shed: life outpoured—atonement and Christian Eucharist (cf. John 6.52-56, etc.).

5. your blood of your lives

That is (in the light of the above remarks) literally, ' your life-blood '. LIFE here (as in v. 4) is properly ' soul '.

will I require

God will avenge murder: the animals may be killed, but their blood must not be eaten; men must not be killed at all, except as penalty for murder.

at the hand of every beast will I require it

This quaint expression means that God commands that every beast which kills a man shall be put to death; cf. Exod. 21.28.

6. by man shall his blood be shed

This verse gives to men the right to put murderers (but no one else) to death; it is not stated how this should be done. In earlier times it was the duty of the next-of-kin (*go'el*, see notes on Gen. 4.10, 15); in later times it is the duty of the State. This verse is very significant, because there is implied in it the setting up of civil government in human society, with power even of life and death. The Bible regards the civil government as divinely instituted and the right to 'bear the sword' as given to the rulers by God. As a commentary upon or amplification of this verse one might read Rom. 13.1-7; I Pet. 2.13-17; I Tim. 2.1-3. It is implied that government is necessary in every race of mankind and in every age, and the setting up of political authority in the world is here traced back to God's covenant with Noah. Government may be a necessary evil, due to the Fall, but it is nevertheless a gracious gift of God's loving care for the world that he has not abandoned. Until God's 'reign' comes, government will always be necessary; when his 'reign' begins, political authority will no longer be required, as it was not required in the original creation as God intended it (cf. I Cor. 15.24). The State will not 'wither away' in this world-age, for it is established by God's 'everlasting covenant' with mankind. Therefore we must obey the duly constituted political authorities as the very 'ministers of God' (Rom. 13.6). The State is ordained by God to restrain lawlessness; rulers must themselves obey God's law and not become capricious despots; 'force is entrusted to the State in order that the State may prevent the lawless use of force' (W. Temple). All this in embryo is implicit in the essentially *biblical* insight embodied in this verse.

for in the image of God made he man

P again insists that the image of God in man was not obliterated by the Fall (cf. 5.3). There is profound insight here. Man's life (soul) is sacred, not because man is valuable in himself (humanism) or because it is itself a 'spark' of the divine life (stoicism, pantheism), but because man is made in God's image and likeness. Nowadays we hear much talk about the 'sacredness of personality', but it is often forgotten that it is only 'God's image in man that implies sacredness, and that where belief in God is lacking respect for human personality does not long survive. Much of P's teaching here is parallel to J's teaching in the story of Cain and Abel: Cain, though a sinner, yet stands under the protection of God and bears the mark of God's solicitude; in P, also, though man is a sinner, the 'mark' of his dignity and the safeguard of his life is still the image of God which remains in him (see notes on 4.9, 15).

7. God's blessing of Noah and his sons ends by repeating (as is P's wont) the dominant theme and phrase.

9. I establish my covenant

See general introduction to this section.

and with your seed after you

P makes it quite clear that he intends the COVENANT with Noah to be understood as God's covenant with the whole human race, Noah's SEED. The next verse shows that he regards it as including not only the human race but all living creatures.

11. neither shall all flesh be cut off

The COVENANT must, of course, not be thought of (as this verse taken by itself would imply) merely as a negative thing, a promise never to destroy the earth again with a catastrophe like the Flood. This verse must be interpreted in the light of vv. 1-7. God promises positively to sustain all life, and he institutes law and government in human society.

12. the token of the covenant

It is usual for a TOKEN or sign to be set up as a symbol and reminder of a COVENANT (see on 4.15, A SIGN FOR CAIN). The TOKEN or sign of God's covenant with Noah (i.e. with mankind) is the BOW IN THE CLOUD (i.e. rainbow), which P apparently thinks of as not having been seen before the Flood. The rainbow which appears after the storm is a fitting and beautiful symbol of God's tender mercy towards mankind: God has laid aside his wrath—he has 'set his bow in the cloud' (the Hebrew word for a war-bow is the same as that for rainbow) and thus put away his instrument of destruction. Here we find biblical sanction for the view that man's 'natural piety' is not misconceived when his heart is uplifted in the presence of this beautiful phenomen of nature (cf. Wordsworth's 'My heart leaps up', or O. Wendell Holmes's 'Lord of all being', *Songs of Praise*, 564). In the biblical symbolism the rainbow appears again only in Ezek. 1.28, where a rainbow (probably a token of mercy) surrounds the Almighty on his throne girt about with fire (an emblem of holiness and judgment), and in Rev. 4.3 and 10.1, where the same symbolism, borrowed from Ezekiel, is intended by the rainbow (Gk. *iris*); at Rev. 6.2 a different Greek word (*toxon*, a war-bow) is used. It is interesting to note that the LXX translators of Gen. 9.13, 14 and 16 render by *toxon*, not *iris*.

16. the everlasting covenant

Note P's stress on the continuing character of the

COVENANT with Noah (i.e., with every living creature). It is
no mere interim-provision until the covenant with Abraham
or the Horeb-Sinai covenant shall be made (cf. also FOR
PERPETUAL GENERATIONS, v. 12). The N.T. writers likewise
do not suppose that it has been abrogated by the New
Covenant (it is conceivable that the so-called 'Noachic'
decree of the Council of Jerusalem, Acts 15.29, was in some
sense intended as a republication of it, but this is too complicated a matter to discuss here). The truth embodied in
the story of the covenant with Noah is that God will remain
for ever the merciful protector and sustainer of all mankind. Though he will make a covenant with Abraham, it
is only in order that in his seed *all* the nations of the earth
shall be blessed (Gen. 22.18); though he will by the Horeb-
Sinai covenant take Israel for 'a peculiar treasure', it is
only in order that Israel may become a kingdom of priests
to all nations ('for all the earth is mine') (Exod. 19.5f.).
And finally God's merciful love to all mankind, of which the
rainbow is a token, will be revealed and made available to
the whole world through the New Covenant in the blood of
Jesus Messiah.

IX

NOAH AND HIS SONS
9.18-27 (J); 28-29 (P)

To modern ears the story of Noah's nakedness is repellent;
was there nothing more edifying that the story-teller could
have found to relate of the 'righteous' Noah after his deliverance? Our answer must be that the 'heroes' of the
Bible are not plaster saints, but flesh-and-blood mortals like
ourselves, sinners in whom God's grace is nevertheless revealed. Even though delivered, blessed and accounted
righteous by God, men are still not perfect; they are still
sinners. But there is a further meaning in the parable, as
we shall see.

18. Shem, and Ham, and Japheth
The three sons of Noah are the fathers of the three great
families of mankind into which the Hebrews divided the
inhabited world as they knew it. SHEM (hence *Semite,
Semitic*) is the true line of God's election (cf. Seth as the
foundation of the Adamic Church, 4.25, and see note on
4.25f.); the true line of descent from SHEM is that of Israel.
HAM is the father of the Egyptians, Ethiopians and Abys-
sinians; but he has a son CANAAN, who is the father of the
Canaanite inhabitants of Palestine whom the invading
Hebrews had dispossessed and subjugated. JAPHETH is the
father of the Gentiles. (See 10.1ff.)

20. Noah . . . planted a vineyard
Noah had to reinstitute husbandry after the Flood, but he

is credited with the invention of viniculture. The Hebrew
tradition on the whole regards wine as good and wholesome,
a blessing from the Lord; but at the same time it is full of
warnings against the immoderate drinking of WINE. The
point of the parable here, however, does not concern the
theme of moderation; it concerns rather the degradation of
pagan (Canaanite) religious orgies of drunkenness practised
in the worship of the fertility-baals. The licentious baal-
religion was a constant temptation to the Israelites in Palestine, and Noah is here represented as falling a victim to it.
The austere worship of Jehovah can have nothing in common with the frenzied intoxication and exhibitionism of the
baal-cults. We cannot understand the true significance of
the curse that is afterwards laid upon Canaan unless we
perceive that this is the symbolic meaning of Noah's
drunkenness.

21. drunken . . . and uncovered

Perhaps we are intended to understand that Noah, being
without experience of the effects of wine, succumbed through
no fault of his own. He lies naked in a drunken stupor.

22. Ham . . . saw the nakedness

To be naked is throughout the O.T. (cf. Gen. 3.7, 10f.,
21) a sign of disgrace and humiliation; to see (even accident-
ally) the NAKEDNESS of one's father was to bring shame and
disgrace upon oneself. Hence the delicate behaviour of
SHEM and JAPHETH in v. 23.

25. Cursed be Canaan

In Hebrew thought a father's blessing or curse was no
mere wish or petition; it was determinative of the future,
having a self-fulfilling potency (cf. Gen. 27; 48.13-20; 49).
The Canaanites with their degenerate and immoral fertility
religion are condemned to be A SERVANT OF SERVANTS (i.e.
the meanest slaves), as indeed they became to the Hebrews

after the conquest of the land. We may ask why CANAAN is cursed for Ham's indiscretion. The answer is that the exigencies of the facts require it: the other Hamitic peoples (Egyptians, etc.) are not regarded as inferiors in the sense that the Canaanites are. The parable had somehow to bring a curse upon CANAAN—that is, not upon an individual, but upon a culture in which religion was synonymous with immorality. The story-teller has little concern for the logicality of his story.

26. Blessed be the LORD, the God of Shem

SHEM means 'name', and the blessing of Israel consisted in the fact that to Israel alone God was known by his proper name, Jehovah.

27. God enlarge Japheth

Noah blesses the Gentiles: ENLARGE (Heb. *yapht*) is a play on the name JAPHETH. It is doubtful what is intended by the clause LET HIM (or, he shall) DWELL IN THE TENTS OF SHEM. The Fathers of the Church read it as a veiled prophecy of the regrafting of the Gentiles into the true stem of Israel (Rom. 11.17). Such a notion could hardly have been present in J's mind, but it may be that he looks forward to the day when the sons of Shem shall be a light to lighten the Gentiles (cf. Isa. 49.6) and the whole world shall call upon the *shem Jahweh*.

28, 29. These verses are from P, and are probably the concluding words of his narrative of the Flood.

X

THE ORIGIN OF
THE NATIONS
10.1-32; P and J

In this chapter, compiled by the editor from his two sources, a fundamental theme of Genesis, and indeed of the whole Bible, is pursued. It is the theme of the selection of Israel out of the great number of the nations of the earth. Gradually the interest of the biblical history narrows from the universality of the covenant with Noah to the particularity of the covenant with Abraham and his seed (Gen. 17); thereafter it records the history of the Chosen People, and then of the faithful Remnant within it, until at last the New Covenant is made and the preaching of the Gospel to 'all nations' (Matt. 28.19; Mark 13.10) begins. Here in Gen. 10 it is implied that God's purpose embraces all the nations, for all are in truth one big family, sprung from a common ancestor. An attempt is made to show the relationship of Israel to the other nations of the earth. After this has been done, the editor can devote his attention exclusively to the true line of development from Shem to Terah, the father of Abraham (11.10-26).

Though cast in the form of a genealogical table, the chapter is concerned not with individuals but with nations. The persons mentioned are eponymous; that is to say, they are persons called into existence to account for the name of a people or country. This was a common phenomenon in the ancient world (cf. Romulus-Rome, Romans; Italus-Italy; Tros-Troy, Trojans; etc.). Thus the relationships of

the persons named are in reality intended to describe the
origins of peoples and their affinities with one another.
Needless to say, the table has little scientific value in the
light of modern ethnology: for example, the Canaanites and
the Egyptians are quite unrelated stocks, and it was only the
close intercourse between Canaan and Egypt in culture and
trade that led the Hebrews to think of Canaan as a ' son '
of Ham.   Often the relationships attributed to different
peoples are thus only geographical and are not relationships
of blood at all.   The surprising thing about the chapter is
the extent of the knowledge of the inhabited world which
the Hebrews possessed.   P's knowledge is wider than J's;
he is acquainted with the peoples of the whole Mediter-
ranean, with Media and Armenia and Nubia, all of which
seem to lie beyond the horizon of J.

Nothing could indicate more clearly than does this chapter
the firmness and antiquity of the Hebrew conviction that
Jehovah is the God of all the earth, the Lord of the nations
and the hope of the Gentiles.   Such a view of God was, we
know, held by the later prophets, notably the Second Isaiah;
in their writings it is explicitly and cogently developed.   But
that the idea of God as the God of the whole earth, the
Lord of history and Saviour of mankind, was not a new discovery of the post-exilic prophets is abundantly proved from
the story of Noah and the appended genealogical tables of
the races of mankind.

The elucidation of all the names in Chapter X would
require a very detailed and technical discussion, such as
cannot be attempted here.   The matter is full of interest for
those equipped with all the necessary philological, archæological and historical knowledge, but it can be dealt with
adequately only on a basis of such knowledge.   In the brief
notes which follow we call attention to a few of the more
obvious points of interest.

FROM P'S TABLE
10.1-7

2. Gomer, Magog . . . Tubal

Peoples from the Black Sea regions. Ezekiel speaks of
an attack to be made upon the restored Israel by MAGOG
(ruled over by their prince Gog) in alliance with GOMER and
TUBAL and other peoples from 'the uttermost parts of the
north' (Ezek. 38.2, 6; 39.1ff.).

Javan, the Ionians, or the Greeks in general.

Madai, the Medes.

3. Togarmah

Also a confederate of Magog in Ezek. 38.6.

4. the sons of Javan

Greek colonists: ELISHAH may be somewhere in Cyprus;
TARSHISH, Gk. *Tartessus*, a Greek colony in Spain near the
mouth of the Guadalquiver, often mentioned in the O.T.
(e.g., I Kings 10.22); KITTIM, the people of Kit (Gk. *Kition*),
in Cyprus (often in O.T.); DODANIM (more correctly with
LXX and Sam., *Rodanim,* RV margin), the Rhodians.
The Greek colonists are people of the 'isles' or 'coasts'
(v. 5).

6. the sons of Ham

CUSH and MIZRAIM are two names for Egypt, as also often
in O.T. is HAM (e.g., Ps. 105.23, 27). PUT is some people
living beside Egypt, possibly the Libyans. CANAAN is the
eponymous ancestor of the inhabitants of Canaan, whom the
Israelites subjugated and regarded as their servants (Gen.
9.25). In point of fact the Canaanites were a Semitic people
whose language was akin to Hebrew; they are not related
to the Egyptians.

7. the sons of Cush

These seem to be tribes in Arabia. SHEBA, i.e., the Sabaeans of S.W. Arabia, are great traders often mentioned in the O.T. (cf. the story of the Queen of Sheba, I Kings 10.1-13). According to J's table (10.28f.) they are descended from Joktan and are not Hamites but Semites.

THE ORIGIN OF THE BABYLONIAN AND ASSYRIAN EMPIRES: NIMROD (J) 10.8-12

The ancient and mighty civilizations of Babylon and Assyria must always have fascinated the Hebrew mind even when they did not threaten Hebrew existence. They are associated with NIMROD, mentioned here only in the O.T. (except Mic. 5.6), and about whom nothing else is known. NIMROD seems to be the only name of an individual (not a people) in this chapter. His character is exactly that of the warrior-king of the Babylonian-Assyrian type, and to him is attributed the origin of the military state which extends its empire by sheer and ruthless force.

8. Cush begat Nimrod

Perhaps the editor mistook CUSH for *Kash*, a people who conquered Babylonia in the eighteenth century B.C. It is improbable that the Hebrew tradition went so far astray as to imagine that the civilizations of Babylon and Nineveh originated in Egypt.

he began to be a mighty one

That is, he was the first to be a *Gibbor* (Heb. 'mighty one'), a military despot. The word has been used of the NEPHILIM in 6.4, but here it does not imply superhuman attributes. NIMROD is the prototype of the 'great man' who by the ruthless and demonic force of his will to power

dominates peoples and empires. We are more familiar with
Napoleon or Hitler, but for the Hebrews the model of this
kind of despot was to be found in Babylon or Nineveh.

9. a mighty hunter before the LORD

The warrior-kings of Babylonia and Assyria loved to
boast their prowess in the chase and are often depicted in
art as victorious in combat with lions, etc. The phrase
'before Jahweh' here is very remarkable. What did this first
despot know of Jahweh? The phrase implies that he lived
consciously in the presence of Jahweh. In the first generations of mankind after Noah the knowledge of God still per-
sisted amongst even the non-Semites—this would seem to be
implied. Furthermore it was this consciousness of Jahweh
which made Nimrod MIGHTY—the first soldier, the first
despot, the first founder of cities and empires. The conception of the demonic (see notes on 6.1-4) meets us again
here, though, of course, J himself did not think of the matter
in such conceptual terms. The 'greatness' of a man or a
nation is indeed based upon God-given qualities and endow-
ments, and yet these very gifts become the instruments by
which men's lust for domination is gratified at the cost of
incalculable suffering and injustice. So it was with Babylon
and Nineveh. About the greatness of their civilization and the
magnitude of their achievement there can be no dispute; yet
in the biblical story these two cities become synonymous
with cruelty, lust, oppression and ruthless power. Yet, even
so, they do not achieve their greatness apart from or in
spite of the will of God; even in the arrogance of their
triumph they are still but instruments in the hand of Jehovah
and will not escape his wrath (cf. Isa. 10.5-15). Forgetting
the knowledge of God which Nimrod possessed, they became exalted in their own heathen pride and oppressors of
God's people; even in N.T. times Babylon still remains a
symbol of cruelty, vice and the lust for power (cf. Rev. 17.5;
18.10, 21). The ultimate biblical word upon the 'mighty

ones' of the world-empires is: 'Thou wouldest have no power against me, except it were given thee from above' (John 19.11).

wherefore it is said, Like Nimrod

J explains how the expression 'So-and-so is like Nimrod' had become a proverbial saying in Israel (cf. I Sam. 10.11f.).

10. the beginning of his kingdom was Babel

BABEL is the Hebrew word for Babylon (which is its Greek form). ERECH, ACCAD and CALNEH are other important cities in Babylonia. SHINAR is a frequent Hebrew name for Babylonia. J does not explicitly say that Nimrod actually founded Babylon, a city which existed centuries before J's time; its earliest known king reigned in the third millennium B.C. J could have little reliable knowledge of so distant a period. But it is probably implied that Nimrod was the founder of Babylon.

11, 12. Nineveh . . . the same is the great city

J does, however, say that Nimrod founded NINEVEH, the capital of Assyria. The other Assyrian cities mentioned are varying distances from NINEVEH, but they are all lumped together with NINEVEH as THE GREAT CITY.

MOSTLY FROM J'S TABLE
10.13-32

Probably vv. 16-18 are an editorial insertion; vv. 20, 22, 23, 31 and 32 are from P; the rest is J.

13, 14. The 'sons' of MIZRAIM are probably parts of Egypt or Egyptian territories. The CAPHTORIM are the inhabitants of Caphtor, probably Crete, thought of as an Egyptian dependency. The redoubtable PHILISTINES, with whom Saul and David struggled, dwelt on the coast of the Mediter-

ranean west of Judah.   They are usually said to have come
from Caphtor (e.g., Amos 9.7) and the words in brackets in
v. 14 should doubtless follow CAPHTORIM, not CASLUHIM.

15-18. The 'sons' of CANAAN, according to J, are ZIDON (i.e.,
the Zidonians or Phœnicians, the seafaring people of the
N.W. coastal strip of Palestine: Tyre and Sidon) and HETH
(i.e., the Hittites, who lived to the north of the Phœnicians
and whose powerful empire lasted from *c*. 1600 B.C. to 700).
To these the editor adds the four peoples of Canaan (Jebus-
ites, whose capital was Jerusalem till David captured it,
II Sam. 5.6-9; Amorites; Girgashites; Hivites) and the inhabitants of five cities (Arkites, etc.) of the Phœnician north.

21-32. Having disposed of the 'sons' of Japheth and Ham,
the editor can now devote his attention to the 'sons' of
SHEM, that is, the tribes which he considered 'Semitic'.
These include the Arabian tribes listed in vv. 25-30 as well
as those that were sprung from the true line of Shem
through Abraham listed in 11.16-26.   Note that the editor
has retained the introduction of J (v. 21) as well as that of
P (v. 22).

21. Eber, the eponymous ancestor of the *Hebrews*, which
seems to have been the name by which other peoples called
the Israelites.   Also in 10.25; 11.14.

Shem . . . the elder brother of Japheth
The editor is working out his scheme of narrowing down
the list of peoples until he finally eliminates all except the
true line through Abraham (11.26 ff., ABRAM).   This is why
he is dealing with Shem's descendants *after* he has dealt
with Japheth's and Ham's.   This order would imply in
Hebrew usage that SHEM was the younger brother, and so
these words (THE ELDER BROTHER OF JAPHETH) are added
(or retained) to make it clear that SHEM is the firstborn.

After interrupting his genealogies in order to insert the story of the Tower of Babel (11.1-9), the editor resumes in 11.10ff. with P's table of the true development from Shem to Abraham. We must not think of all these genealogical tables in Gen. 10 and 11 as dull lists of names, devoid of interest because they possess no historical value, nor yet as possessing interest only for scholars and antiquarians because of the light they throw upon ancient ethnological beliefs. They have a profound theological significance which is germane to the theme of the Bible as a whole. The Bible tells the story of our redemption: God redeemed mankind by means of his historical selection of a people to be the instrument of his purpose. That people becomes a Church within the world; then God's purpose is carried forward by means of a remnant within that Church, until finally the true Israel is narrowed down to a single individual, the Messiah Jesus. When at last all his disciples have forsaken him and fled, he stands alone—the sole representative of the Israel of God—and alone he becomes the instrument of God's salvation of all the sons of Noah, the uncountable races sprung from Shem, Ham and Japheth, out of which are called the great multitude which no man could number, of all nations and tribes and peoples and tongues, who cry with a great voice, 'Salvation unto our God and unto the Lamb' (Rev. 7.9f.).

XI

THE TOWER OF BABEL

11.1-9; J

This remarkable parable contains much more than 'the answer which Hebrew folk-lore gave to the question which differences of language directly suggested' (Driver). It contains in story-form the essential biblical verdict upon secular civilization, represented in the parable by the city and tower of Babel—that Babylon which throughout the Bible remains the symbol of man's megalomaniacal attempt to achieve world peace and unity by world domination and exploitation (see on 10.9). The good and the bad are so mixed in human nature that man's noblest aspirations and achievements become the source of his defiance of God and oppression of his neighbour. Pride—which is always pride in something that is good, some capacity, some achievement—is the basic sin (see on 3.4); in the parable THE WHOLE EARTH desires to MAKE A NAME—and so it happens that man seeks to set up his name as a rival name to the *shem Jahweh*, to which alone praise and glory properly belong. (Cf. in the parable of the Fall the desire of Adam to be 'as God', 3.5.) Man seeks by his own virtue and cleverness to BUILD A TOWER WHOSE TOP MAY REACH TO HEAVEN, to erect a civilization that recks little of God's grace and therefore of his law. Such civilizations—from the military state to the welfare state, if they judge themselves able to dispense with God's grace and law—are doomed to end in catastrophe and confusion. In the language of the parable, God 'comes down' from heaven—in judgment upon secular civilization. But

124

this does not mean that God is only a God of wrath, or that he seeks to thwart the good intentions of men in ordering the affairs of secular life. God's judgment is always judgment on man's pride. The Bible goes on to tell how God ' came down from heaven ' in mercy, not only in judgment, in order to seek and to save that which was lost. But to receive this offer of unmerited salvation men must deny their pride, renounce their Babel presumptuousness, and accept God's gift ' as little children '. The ' saints ', alike of the O.T. and the N.T., are those who indeed seek a city, but it is not one which they can build till its towers reach heaven; it is a city whose builder and maker is God (Heb. 11.10).

The parable thus sets before us recurring biblical themes. One of them is that of the overweening pride of towering cities (states, empires). Now one city, now another, becomes the *type* of man's reckless defiance of God's purpose and law—Sodom and Gomorrah, the habitations of unnatural vice (Gen. 18, 19); Tyre, whose amazing commercial prosperity spelt luxury for the few and exploitation for the many (Ezek. 26-28); Babylon, the military despotism which enslaved the peoples of many races and lands. And Babylon becomes the prototype of all the cities and empires of the world that despise God's grace and law; as at the beginning of the Bible Babylon is raised in pride and brought down in confusion, so at the end of the Bible it is Babylon—even though now Babylon stands for Imperial Rome—whose hour of judgment is come. The author of the Apocalypse clearly has the parable of Gen. 11.1-9 in his mind when he writes: ' Thus with a mighty fall shall Babylon, the great city, be cast down, and shall be found no more at all ' (Rev. 18.21).

Another biblical theme encountered in the parable is that of the unity of mankind, shattered by reason of man's sin. The Bible tells the story of God's plan to recreate the lost unity of the human family. In Genesis we read of all mankind as originally one family, the sons of Noah, and of the

differentiation of mankind into all the many races and
kindreds of the earth. The parable of the Tower of Babel
emphasizes that it is man's exaltation of himself as over
against God which is the prime cause of divisions and
rivalries, of which the different languages are symbolic.
Men cannot speak to one another in a common tongue
because they have no common interest or mutual regard.
God seeks to recreate mankind into one great family, the
universal Church, united in one covenant of love in the
blood of Jesus Christ, and speaking one common language
of the Holy Spirit of God. The story of Pentecost, with its
miraculous reversal of the Babel confusion of languages,
is itself a parable of the power of the divine love to bind
together 'men from every nation under heaven' in the New
Covenant of grace (Acts 2.5-11); the story of the Gift of
Tongues at Pentecost is nothing other than the Babel story
in reverse. When men in their pride boast of their own
achievements, there results nothing but division, confusion
and incomprehensibility; but when the wonderful works of
God are proclaimed, then every man may hear the apostolic
Gospel in his own tongue.

The parable of the Tower of Babel, though it undoubtedly
emanates from within the J stream of traditional material,
seems to bear little connection with J's genealogy and is not
entirely consistent with it. The genealogy seems to account
for differences of nation and language by showing how the
families of the earth multiplied and formed different ethnic
groups with different customs and traditions in different
parts of the earth over a long period of time. The Babel
parable accounts for differences of race and language as the
result of a single divine intervention at a particular moment
of history. But we must remember that the parable is not
seeking to give us literal history—at least in its present form
in our Bibles. Doubtless those who first told this story in
primitive times held it to be a description of what had really
happened and of how the divisions of mankind arose. But

the J writer (or his editor) sets it forward for our learning not as a true story, but as a parable of the encounter of sinful humanity with the God of righteousness. It is a story of the 'Fall' type, such as we have noted the stories of Cain and Abel, the Fallen Angels and the Flood also were. We cannot say what was its relation to the other J material; it seems to know nothing of the tradition that Babylon was founded by Nimrod. That the story has had a long history in the oral tradition before our editor gave it its present shape is obvious. Indeed, more than fifty years ago, Gunkel very plausibly suggested that the editor has in fact fashioned our story out of two distinct traditions, one of which related the founding of a city, the other the building of a tower (see Skinner, I.C.C., p. 223). But however it assumed its present form its biblical meaning as it now stands is not obscure.

2. as they journeyed
The WHOLE EARTH is thought of as living and moving in one great company of nomads.

Shinar, Babylonia; cf. 10.10.

4. a city
Babylon, as we learn in v. 9.

a tower, whose top may reach unto heaven
The Hebrews thought of the sky (firmament) as the floor of heaven (see on 1.6) and it was not so very far above the earth. Theoretically there could be no reason why, if one went on piling bricks on top of one another, one should not eventually build a tower whose top might reach heaven. The story as it now stands is, of course, a parable, and the TOWER represents secular civilization; but it was doubtless fashioned out of an ancient legend concerning the origin of a Babylonian *zikkurat*, a massive pyramidal tower which ascended in terraces and had a temple at the top.

make us a name

Men are strange compounds of both the fear and the love of anonymity. In all men there is present the desire to be famous—by fair means or by foul. The pre-exilic Hebrews had no belief in a truly personal survival of death (but only the forgotten existence of Sheol), and the way to become 'immortal' was to leave behind one a 'name'—fame, reputation, honour, renown (cf. Ecclus. 44.1-15). The hatred of anonymity drives men to heroic feats of valour or long hours of drudgery; or it urges them to spectacular acts of shame or of unscrupulous self-preferment. In its worst forms it tempts men to give the honour and glory to themselves which properly belong to the name of God. Man's concern to make for himself a name leads to the grossest presumptuousness and to the dishonouring or even denial of the name of God.

lest we be scattered abroad

Perhaps in some early version of the story a reason for building the tower was to create a landmark which, being as high as heaven, would be visible from every part of the earth. It would thus serve as a rallying point and focus of unity for all mankind. The Bible teaches that there can be no man-made unity, no human device that can restore the lost unity of mankind and become the basis of permanent peace on earth. The 'Covenant' of the League of Nations was the first treaty of the modern world which omitted the name of God from its preamble; the sad history of the League, with its ending in confusion and scattering, is perhaps a modern version of the Tower of Babel. There are many other parallels in history.

5. the LORD came down to see

Here again we find the anthropomorphic language that is characteristic of J (cf. 3.8; 8.21, etc.).

6. and now nothing will be withholden

This verse is reminiscent of 3.22f. There, as here, it is not intended that God should be thought of as jealously preventing the progress of mankind in order to preserve his own supremacy; it is implied that God in his wisdom finds means of checking the presumptuous ambitions of men which cannot lead them to their God-appointed destiny.

7. let us go down

For the use of the plural (LET US) in connection with the being of God see note on *Elohim*, 1.1.

confound their language

The inability of one people to understand the language of another is indicative of the lack of truly human intercourse. Wherever common interests (even those of mutual trade) establish relationships between peoples, the barriers of language are broken down. Community of interest is destroyed by the desire of the different peoples to 'make a name' for themselves—by domination, exploitation or even extermination of other peoples. This is peculiarly the sin of Babylon, but it is the sin of all peoples everywhere. The parable is near the truth in suggesting that the confusion of language is a consequence and symbol of men's desire to make a name for themselves. Can men overcome this confusion of speech by artificially creating a common language, such as Esperanto? At any rate it is a matter for reflection that a common language (*lingua franca*) has existed in history only when some great military and economic power has established community of interests over a wide area and left (after it has vanished) a widely understood language behind it (cf. Greek in the time of our Lord, long after the Greek domination established by Alexander the Great had passed away, or the English language to-day, especially in India and the Far East).

9. therefore was the name of it called Babel

Actually the etymological meaning of the name of Babylon is 'gate of God' (Bab-El), which might fittingly have served as a text for a story about a tower to heaven! But the Hebrew narrator saw the opportunity for a play upon words in the Hebrew word *balal*, to mix or confuse (RV margin).

XII

GENEALOGY FROM SHEM
TO ABRAM (ABRAHAM)

11.10-32; mostly P

Having disposed of the many races and tribes of the earth,
all of whom are included in the covenant with Noah, the
editor is now able to concentrate attention upon the true
line of development from SHEM, the people specially chosen
by God as those through whom he will glorify his name.
The names in this section, taken from P's genealogical table,
convey little to us—at least until we reach v. 24. They suggest that a long interval of time has elapsed between the
Flood and the birth of Abraham (290 years according to the
Hebrew text, but longer in the LXX and the Samaritan
recensions). We may notice that as we move further away
from the creation the duration of the lives of the patriarchs,
though still of abnormal length, is becoming shorter in
accordance with P's theory (see introductory note to 5.1-32).

14-16. Eber

EBER is the eponymous ancestor of the Hebrews (see on
10.21). As in 10.25 (J) the P genealogist assumes that there
were Hebrew tribes that were not of the true line of development from Eber through PELEG to Abraham.

26. Terah . . . begat Abram, Nahor and Haran

It is difficult to say at what point the names in Genesis
cease to be simply the personification of tribes and become
the proper names of individuals. That there was a real

person called Abraham, who had a son Isaac, and concerning whom the traditions contained in Chapters 12ff. have been collected, can hardly be doubted; it is very difficult to continue after Chapter 12 upon the assumption that Abraham, Isaac and Jacob are merely personifications of tribal movements and histories. ABRAM is, of course, Abraham, whose name was changed to this more familiar form according to the story in 17.5. ABRAM, which is a contraction of Abiram, means 'the [divine] father is exalted'; *Abraham* has no known etymology, but in 17.5 it is explained by a play on words as meaning 'the father of a multitude of nations' (Heb. *hamon*, a multitude).

27. the generations of Terah

Presumably we are to understand that the Terahites divided into three sections, the Abramites, Nahorites and Haranites. The Haranites, however, passed out of existence as a distinct tribe, but there was a surviving branch called Lot.

28-30. These verses are an editorial insertion from J and anticipate stories included in Chapters 12ff.

31. they went forth with them

The LXX and Samaritan versions read 'he brought them forth from Ur', which is clearly what is meant. The Terahites led the dependent Abramites and the Lot tribe on a migration from Babylonia towards Palestine.

Ur of the Chaldees

The city of UR was important long before the rise of Babylon; it is 125 miles from the mouth of the Euphrates. This tradition implies that the Hebrews originally came from Ur in the south of Babylonia, but it is not the only tradition on the subject, since there is evidence in J of a Mesopotamian origin. We may leave the question to the experts. The CHALDEES (Bab. and Ass. *Kaldu*, Heb. *Kasdim*, Gk. *Chaldaioi*, whence *Chaldees*, or *Chaldeans*, often in EVV of the prophets) are the Babylonians; more precisely they were a tribe of southern Babylonia who at a later date became the ruling caste in Babylonia (under Nabopolassar, 625-605 B.C., and Nebuchadrezzar, 604-561).

Haran

A city of considerable importance in Mesopotamia. The word is properly *Charan* (perhaps meaning ' cross-roads ') and is not the same word as Haran (soft H), Terah's son (vv. 26ff.). Both UR and HARAN were notable centres of moon-worship and there is evidence that some of the Hebrew tribes were at one stage of their development influenced by a cult of the moon. The word Laban means ' moon ' (cf. ' Laban the son of Nahor ' in Gen. 29.5).

32. Terah died in Haran

The leadership of the migratory Hebrews passed to the Abramites during their sojourn in Mesopotamia; presumably the Terahites passed out of existence as a distinct and recognizable tribe. The scene is now set for the story of the Call of Abraham and his migration from Mesopotamia to Canaan (12.1ff.).

At this point the first part of the Book of Genesis ends. The second part (12.1ff.), which contains the patriarchal narratives, deals with the making by God of a nation, Israel, which shall carry forward his purpose of the salvation of the world. The first part deals with the origin and development of all the tribes and kindreds of the earth; and the covenant about which it tells us is the covenant with Noah. The second part concentrates attention upon the single nation which God has called to be his instrument; and the covenant about which we there read is the covenant with ' faithful Abraham ', the father of the chosen people. But there is no difference of interest or outlook between the two parts of Genesis, just as there is no contradiction between the two covenants. The concern of Gen. 1-11 with the multiplicity of nations and tribes, their origin and development, is no mere childish curiosity about foreign peoples and lands; it is a concern for the human race in the purpose of God. The concern of Gen. 12ff. with the true line of Abraham does not mean that the former interest in 'the whole earth' has been forgotten; on the contrary, Abraham is called and blessed in order that God's purpose for the human race as such may be realized: 'in thy seed shall *all* the nations of the earth be blessed' (Gen. 22.18). Genesis, in fact, in both its parts anticipates the later prophetic teaching that God's purpose embraces all the nations and that Israel is elected not for special privileges but to bear the responsibility of being the light to lighten the Gentiles. The covenant with Abraham implements and fulfils the covenant with Noah. But the covenant with Abraham is itself not fulfilled until in the fullness of time 'Abraham's blessing came upon the Gentiles in Christ Jesus' (Gal. 3.14). The Book of Genesis in both its parts looks forward to the realization in Christ of God's plan for mankind, the fulfilment of the covenants both with Noah and with Abraham. Thus Genesis is essentially a *biblical* book: it 'preaches the Gospel beforehand' in its confident proclamation, 'In thy seed shall all the nations of the earth be blessed' (cf. Gal. 3.8). It is biblical because it points forward to Christ; it cannot be understood apart from its fulfilment in Christ. Genesis is a *beginning* whose end is Christ.